999

Inside Death Row in the United States

ISBN : 978-2-31501-255-8
Maps: copyright ECPM
Max Milo Éditions, Paris, 2023
www.maxmilo.com

ARNAUD GAILLARD

999

INSIDE DEATH ROW IN THE UNITED STATES

This book is the result of a fact-finding mission by the association Ensemble contre la peine de mort (ECPM), led by Mr. Arnaud Gaillard under the direction of ECPM. This mission is part of a series of investigations into death rows in Rwanda, Burundi and the DRC (the latter received the French Republic's Human Rights Prize in 2005). ECPM initiated the creation of the World Coalition Against the Death Penalty and organizes the World Congress Against the Death Penalty every three years.

Visit ECPM at www.abolition.fr

"This document has been produced with the financial assistance of the European Union. The contents of this document are the sole responsibility of the author and can in no way be taken to reflect the views of the European Union."

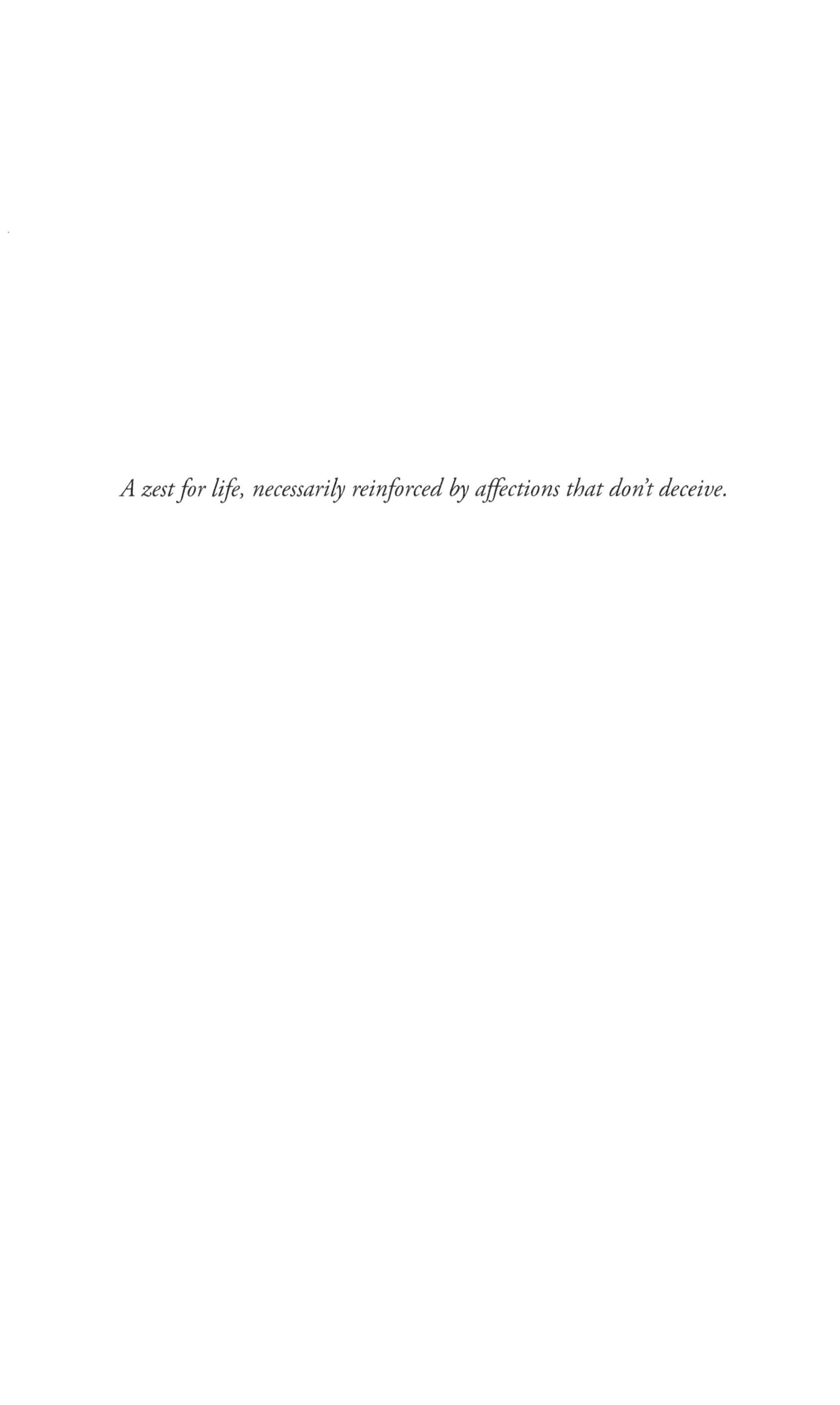

A zest for life, necessarily reinforced by affections that don't deceive.

Foreword

It's not uncommon to hear that the United States, far from leaving people indifferent, is a nation that generates feelings diametrically divided between love and hate. It's as if everything about this country encourages passionate excess. In the view presented here, it's not so much a question of personal feelings, alien to a sociological approach, as of a genuine analysis of a penal phenomenon embodied by a death penalty still present in 34 states. I am perfectly aware, however, that the empirical research that justifies the lines that follow suggests that this essay would be excessively harsh on this great country, its culture, its people and its generous paradoxes. However, as opposed to casting anathema on the New World in its entirety, I urge readers to temper their impression by resituating the true point of view developed here. The entire narrative and all the analyses that follow are based on the prism of the criminal justice system, and capital punishment. This approach should suffice to weigh this book down, since its purpose is not to discuss the United States in an absolute and exhaustive manner, but rather to understand the meaning and functioning of a sentence that all other democracies in the world - with the exception of Japan and India - have chosen to consign to the side of barbarism and the past. Whether we look at the personal histories of all the individuals concerned by the death penalty, whether we incorporate the figures, or observe the more factual aspects of capital punishment in the heart of the states that maintain it, in all cases, the analysis can only generate radical conclusions, which local actors do not fail to observe. Looking at the United States through the prism of the death penalty, the judicial system, living conditions on death row, and the cultural and historical justifications that underpin this situation, certainly leads to the emergence of an extremely violent vision of this country. However, in the face of these penal situations, which are frequently more a matter of torture than justice, any timidity in expressing the context observed in 2010 would be counter-productive. Following the example of a number of publications, often based on quantitative analyses, but revealing the same reality, we must be able to put the lie to the all-too-frequently uttered phrase: "We didn't know…" That's why the ambition of these pages is to help us see and understand.

American abolitionist associations, as well as lawyers, most of whom are court-appointed, are well aware of my conclusions. In fact, there is a large body of work[1] that examines the workings of capital punishment, most often based on numerical data, highlighting discrimination, the financial inequity between defense and prosecution, and a whole range of statistical data that have fed into the mainly qualitative analysis of this essay. This is why, in order not to repeat the undeniable effectiveness of work already carried out, but also because this reflection was conducted from a local field, the choice fell on a form of sociological curiosity to translate into words the eloquence already known by the figures. In this way, I hope that these pages will bring to people's consciences a greater capacity for understanding and contextualization, to further the struggle for a justice that will, one day soon, cease to kill.

---

1. The Death Penalty Information Center (www.deathpenaltyinfo.org) brings together the majority of publications on the death penalty in the USA. More specifically on Texas, The StandDown Texas Project, based in Austin (www.standdown.typepad. com), also brings together an astronomical amount of information, studies and links to keep abreast of capital punishment issues.

In contrast to a purely Eurocentric viewpoint, the conclusions of this analysis are based on and legitimized by a dense empirical approach, in terms of encounters, methods and geographical coverage. Eight states were visited, some fifty interviews were conducted, some of them using semi-directive questionnaires, and participant observations were carried out in many strata of American society, well beyond the specific context of penalties. These encounters were supplemented by questionnaires filled in anonymously by death row inmates.

CHAPTER 1:
THE DEMONS OF A NATION

Rarely do citizens realize that behind the arm of justice, as it is conceived and practiced, behind the arm of strength and knowledge, there is the State. A power that must ensure its continuity, for a powerful nation as a federal or state entity. Crudely speaking, under certain regimes, the death penalty unequivocally embodies the power of decision-makers. More covertly, like Max Weber's conclusions on the "monopoly of legitimate violence"[2], behind institutions with pompous titles and subtle philosophies, the death penalty everywhere retains the same virtues, in democracy as elsewhere. It is on the basis of this denial, on the fringes of a relative ignorance maintained by the population, between the inertia of timid curiosity and unshakeable faith in its institutions, that abolition in the United States has still not been achieved at the dawn of the 21st century.

In the light of international standards on incarceration, but also of the general principles of justice in a democratic country, the death penalty, in this case in the United States, is analyzed here as a polymorphous torture. It's not so much a question of the torments of execution as an *instant of putting to death*, certainly in all cases violent and painful. It's

---

2. WEBER (Max), *The Theory of Social and Economic Organization*, New York, The Free Press, 1st edition, 1964, p. 154.

about all that precedes in terms of conditions of confinement, castrated prospects, random judicial recourse, lack of indulgence and faith in beings whom life nonetheless educates. It's a political and legal lie to a society that prefers to keep quiet about other options that might help prevent violence, and sometimes even cure it. It's a dangerous game we play with death, which we expect to have expiatory virtues, which we provoke and which imposes mourning, and over which it's probably wise not to grant ourselves any rights. It's a punishment that plays with time and wear, "asceticizing" desires, to fill life with nothingness, humiliating submission, solitude and imposed despair.

Undoubtedly, torture is also defined by emotions, by a mental certainty that suffers from neither word nor legal structure. Pain is not always acute. It is sometimes throbbing with random peaks, like a litany of abuse that intrudes on bodies and minds. From the discomfort of claustration, from the infinite expectation fed by often blissful optimism or realistic pessimism, from the sensation that individual destinies are held in the hands of sorcerers' apprentices in the mask of vigilantes, from the uselessness of so much imposed suffering, comes the feeling of being the plaything of executioners with vested interests. The latter have many faces and sometimes uniforms. Their responsibilities are divided and subdivided. Only their consciences know what blind and deaf voters prefer to ignore.

It would be a mistake to summarize the United States in terms of these pages. This analysis is based not only on bibliographical sources on national practices, but also on empirical research *through* interviews, questionnaires, observations and immersion in the following states: California, Utah, Oklahoma, Texas, Mississippi, Tennessee and Pennsylvania[3]. Out of 50 states, 16 are abolitionist[4], 34 still execute, of

---

3. But also questionnaires from Virginie.

4. The last state to abolish the death penalty was Illinois. Ratification of the abolition text was voted on March 9, 2011, resulting in the commutation of 15 death sentences to life imprisonment.

which 8 have executed fewer than 2 people since 1976, when capital punishment was reintroduced. On the other hand, even if not all the states making up the USA are retentionist, it should be added that federal legislation does not impose anything on the federated states (except in the context of Supreme Court decisions), and national political discourse officially refrains from changing the debate. Federal and military courts still retain capital punishment as part of their criminal law.

Even if all the death row inmates interviewed persist in feeling hopeful about the final outcome, despite the accumulation of years, everyone - and much more so than society at large - is aware that, time and again, states have probably executed innocent people, and that judicial remedies, the only sources of optimism, will one day run out. Paradoxically, this fear is compounded by the reality that the majority of convicts will die in these hostile jails before being executed. Be that as it may, the death sentence, because it removes any enviable prospect, constitutes a form of torture skilfully distilled year after year. Because it denies and hinders the movement of living beings, both physical and cerebral, because it plays with the scope of an existence by summing up beings in terms of what they have done in a sometimes distant past, the death penalty constitutes a denial of humanity that American society will strive to disguise in order to better fit into a landscape that claims to be modern. Unlike in other countries, or in certain American states[5] where capital punishment is rarely applied, and executions are rare, in the heart of death row in many states[6], the death penalty is a reality that must be tamed in order to survive.

---

5. Wyoming, Nebraska, Idaho, Oregon, Connecticut, Colorado, New Hampshire and Kansas have executed fewer than two people since executions resumed in 1976. *State Execution Data Rates*, Death Penalty Information Center, April 17, 2009.

6. Oklahoma, Texas, Virginia, Missouri, Florida, Georgia, Ohio, Arizona, North Carolina, Alabama, Louisiana, South Carolina, Arkansas, are states that have executed more than 20 people since executions resumed in 1976. *State Execution Data Rates*, Death Penalty Information Center, April 17, 2009.

The United States represents an idea, an icon that conveys a fantasy of freedom and justice. "During the Cold War, the United States thought about abolishing the death penalty in order to show itself, by contrast, more worthy than the USSR," says criminology professor Steven F. Shatz. Shatz. This is still a contemporary vow, to legitimize the lessons in democracy given outside American borders. The United States wants to appear as a humane country, in contrast to others such as Iran and Iraq. For four years (1972-1976), the United States observed a moratorium likely to give hope to the least convinced abolitionists. By legal means, on a constitutional scale, the very idea of capital punishment could have been repudiated in the same way as violence that had become impossible to bear was relegated to the past. The 8th Constitutional Amendment prohibits cruel or unusual punishment, and the 14th specifies that states may not take the lives of citizens without giving them a fair trial. It was on these grounds that a moratorium was imposed by the U.S. Supreme Court in 1972, in Furman[7] v. State of Georgia. Immediately, state legislators, eager to save the legality of the death penalty, redrew the conditions for its application, until another federal Supreme Court decision, "Gregg v. State of Georgia" in 1976[8], confirmed the constitutionality of the death penalty, surrounding its application with details making it "more digestible" from a legal point of view. These decisions were, and remain, political. They responded to the wishes of a majority hungry for blood, hangings, electrocutions, rales and staged finitudes. As Steve Hall, director of the StandDown Texas Project[9], points out: "People in this country are thirsty for punishment. For several decades, the United States has incarcerated more people than any other country in the world." So many sentiments and opinions based on collective fears, the need for vengeance, and

---

7. "Furman v. Georgia, 408 U.S. 238 - (June 29, 1972) - U.S. Supreme Court.

8. 1976 was therefore a pivotal year in the consideration of the contemporary death penalty from a judicial, procedural and quantitative point of view.

9. StandDown Texas Project is a *think tank* that focuses on identifying and promoting best practices in criminal justice.

widespread ignorance authorizing an almost obscurantist faith in the justice system. It is this bitter observation that prevails with vigor today. Conclusions that temper the undeniable passion aroused by this country and its people. Hence the wish, shared by abolitionists the world over and nurtured by a vigorous, tactical and strategic movement of American activists, to see this eminently prescriptive country, this exciting nation, turn its back on its demons in the foreseeable future, irrevocably and without regret.

Chapter 2:
The Unequal Situation of States

On an international level, we can observe that the abolitionist process unfolded according to a progression, with certain stages sometimes overlooked, while others marked the supposed definitive halt of the movement. The United States is unique in that it is a federal nation, made up of federated states whose respective structures resemble independent sovereignties in many respects, and whose governor would represent, by analogy, the equivalent of a Prime Minister. Consequently, although the general principles of state law are governed by the U.S. Constitution, of which the federal Supreme Court remains guarantor, each state has its own legal standards: Constitution, Civil Code, Criminal Code and rules of procedure. This is why any attempt at generalization would deny the singularities that mean justice is definitely not dispensed in the same way from one state to another. For example, 34 of the 50 federal states have retained the death penalty as part of their penal system. In practice, this situation gives rise to very varied use of the death penalty. Some carry out executions every year, while others have retained capital punishment only as an exceptional or symbolic measure. These distinctions are crucial when it comes to understanding, from a global perspective, the advocates of abolition on a national scale. It would be wrong not to consider these differences in the implementation of abolition strategies, and it would be dishonest to associate the American people as a whole, or the elected officials who govern them, with the over-representation of the Southern states. Hence the need for a kind of typology that makes it possible to assess the stages of evolution of the abolitionist process.

Stage 1 is when the legislation authorizing the death penalty in the penal system is applied, today as in the past, rigorously and without wavering, even accelerating in some cases. It's a neutral stage in which abolitionist developments have neither influence nor influence. This is the situation in Texas, Virginia, Florida, Georgia, Alabama, Oklahoma and Ohio, for example.

Stage 2 is when legislation is enacted to reduce the number of cases where the death penalty is applied, and executions are carried out only in extremely exceptional circumstances (less than one execution every 10 years). This is the stage when faith in the death penalty is lost. This is also the stage when the death penalty is at its most symbolic. Its sparing use generates an aura that draws cathartic energy from its rarity, in response to a feeling of collective and individual vengeance, for the most serious crimes[10]. Among the states involved are: Washington (State) (5)[11], Nebraska (3), Montana (3), Pennsylvania (3), Kentucky (3), Oregon (2), Colorado (1), Connecticut (1), Idaho (1), South Dakota (1), Wyoming (1). There's also the Federal Government (3).

Stage 3, known as the "moratorium" stage, is a time of doubt, assumed or not, but present nonetheless. This is the stage when countries doubt their abolitionist convictions, or their ability to impose them. In the United States, this is currently the case in California with its questioning of lethal injection, even if the outcome seems to be a return to executions. This was also the case in New Mexico,

---

10. The definition of "serious crimes" remains variable. Generally speaking, they involve particularly vulnerable victims and/or particularly trying circumstances, both in the occurrence of the crime and in its execution. These are the parameters that will fuel the media's effectiveness as well as society's emotions.

11. Number of executions since the reintroduction of capital punishment in 1976.

where Governor Bill Richardson preferred to suspend executions, then abolish them when he realized that the judicial system was flawed. The same is true of Maryland.

Stage 4 is abolition for ordinary crimes. This is the stage of mature, determined choice. A choice imposed on a majority of the population, the number of retentionists will decrease with the renewal of generations and the awakening of young people in an abolitionist state. In the USA, this situation applies to: Alaska (1957)[12], Hawaii (1948), Illinois (2011), Iowa (1965), Maine (1887), Massachusetts (1984), Michigan (1846), Minnesota (1911), New Jersey (2007), New Mexico (2009), New York (2004), North Dakota (1973), Rhode Island (1984), Vermont (1964), West Virginia (1965), Wisconsin (1853), District of Columbia (1981).

Stage 5 is the ultimate lock-in at all legislative levels and for all types of crime in all circumstances. This is the stage of ethical certainty, of radical determination to get rid of a prerogative that will never again belong to a civilized society. In the United States, this stage of maturation is nowhere to be seen.

If we take a global look at the United States, it's clear that this country, one of the beacons of a certain democratic conception, remains at an early stage in the abolitionist process. Some retentionist states are at stage 1, or between stage 1 and stage 2, while others are between stages 2 and 3. Stage 5 will never be fully achieved until the federal state has evolved. Among the avenues that raise doubts, not about the usefulness but about the nature of the act, the spectacle of the barbarity of certain executions, combined with a heightened awareness of situations in which innocent people have been executed, leads us to lay the foundations for a debate that is not sufficiently open to generate answers, at least for the time of a moratorium. This

---

12. Year of abolition.

development, and the strategies that govern it, require a detailed assessment of the cultural underpinnings of the death penalty in the United States, in order to answer the question as to the hopes and appeasement expected by the population through the death sentence

Death penalty and methods of execution by state as of September 1st, 2011[13]

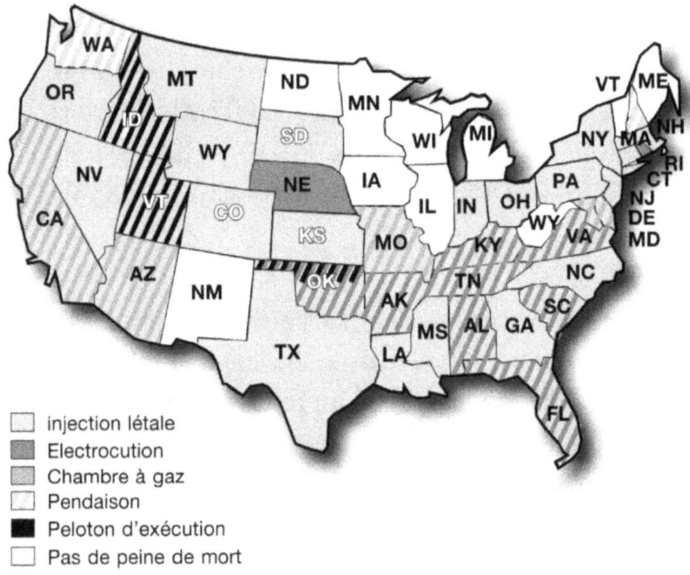

13. All states use lethal injection as their primary method of execution, and most have an alternative method. Firing squad - in Utah for inmates who chose it before it was abolished. The U.S. military and the federal government also authorize execution by lethal injection.

CHAPTER 3:
CULTURAL AND SOCIETAL PORTRAIT OF A YOUNG COUNTRY

The cultural context of the United States is not without interest when it comes to understanding the retention of the death penalty in the 21st century. Because the point here is not to understand capital punishment as an additional disorder expected in a country with a chaotic social and political situation, it is essential to identify aspects of a structured society on which the sentence rests and is argued. We need to understand, through all the moral presuppositions that govern American society, how killing in the name of justice can have a place that is legitimized intellectually and morally. The death penalty in the United States endures only because it rests on an ideological, legal, historical and societal construct, which authorizes all its supporters to defend it. It is in this sense that capital punishment in a democracy relies on a series of specific factors, like so many antidotes to its abolition, which we would normally be entitled to expect in the 21st century in a developed country. In a legalist democracy, a state governed by the rule of law, it is no longer customary to carry out executions. To gain acceptance for this idea, to justify and defend it, opinions and discourses are fed by a complex panorama that must be identified if we hope to sow any hope of abolition. Capital punishment in the United States is not the product of chaos or dictatorial power. It is in every way argued to satisfy, on the one hand, ideas of liberty, justice and law, and on the other, desires for punishment, severity, retribution, fantasies of deterrence and ambitions for efficiency. The result is a series of contradictions, a perverse relationship with reality and with power, which on a day-to-day basis justifies a sentence from another era, while remaining within the national norms of "political correctness". In the United States, therefore, there is a breeding ground for inertia in the face of this civilizational evolution that most other democracies have completed. We cannot reasonably imagine abolishing or dealing with the death penalty without addressing these aspects, perhaps summed up by the ambivalence described in this analysis by Curtis McCarty, an exonerated death row inmate: "In theory, the politicians want the guards to be very hard on us, especially at the time of executions. They defend the usefulness of the sentence; that's what they get elected on. But in fact, they're trying to make things simpler for everyone. I think they remember, somewhere deep down, that you have to respect human beings, they learned that at school, from their mother, from the Church."

The aim of this essay is to explore this ambivalence, which underpins an intellectual and cultural conflict when, on the one hand, the virtues of a sentence are defended, while, on the other, consciences and rationality invalidate it. American history, but also and above all a look at today's society, alive and making decisions, is essential if we are to grasp the unprecedented inertia in a country capable of spectacular renewal in other respects. Instead of existing or disappearing in a masterly social indifference, as is the case in the heart of countries in which political decisions are de facto installed in defiance of the vox populi, the death penalty in the United States is closely interwoven with the foundations of antagonisms arising from historical and cultural aspects that need to be approached. The democratic development of the United States, with elective principles at many levels of the social and institutional structure, requires politicians to satisfy the visions of the majority of voters, including the most counter-productive. Elected representatives either trade in the death penalty as a security tool, or remain discreetly retentionist on principle, particularly for the most violent crimes, i.e. those that move people the most. This is the view of an assertive patriot, a former Navy and General Motors man, who found out the hard way how his country's political and judicial system works, after his only son spent 22 years on death row in Oklahoma, only to be exonerated: "The judicial system itself is great [...] especially being judged by our peers, but the people who work in it are bad, corrupt. There's a District Attorney[14] here, he's sent more people to death row than anyone else, they're even going to make a movie about him."

In the U.S., as elsewhere, it's the emotional criterion that determines the seriousness of crime, associated with rarity, with what's out of the ordinary, with the criminal exceptions with which personalities identify. These specific forms of violence are also abundantly nurtured by cinema and TV series. This publicity, which generates emotions around the crime committed, justifies the individualization of capital punishment, understood as exceptional, in response to what Tocqueville[15] defined as the response to violence suffered. It is also the cathartic value of the death sentence which, independently of any rational basis, represents a totem, murderous to be sure, but ideally perceived as endowed with soothing virtues.

Public opinion

It's not easy to give a collective opinion on the death penalty. On the one hand, it's an infrequent question, and on the other, since the recent emergence of the abolitionist debate, there has been no popular or institutional consensus. Unlike in France and other

---

14. Generally speaking, District Attorneys are state prosecutors elected by district (which may include one or more counties) for a four-year term. They share the Public Prosecutor's Office with federal *prosecutors*, who are appointed by the President of the United States. Their appointments must then be approved by the U.S. Congress. District Attorneys prosecute felonies and misdemeanors under the state's criminal code, while the US Attorney prosecutes felonies and misdemeanors under federal law. Occasionally, there are cases that fall under both jurisdictions, resulting in a state AND a federal trial.

15. TOCQUEVILLE (Alexis de), *Democracy in America*, Paris, Gallimard, 1986.

European countries, where, in educated circles, being in favor of the death penalty is now a politically incorrect idea, in the United States and in the same circumstances, at the end of every discussion, the interlocutors we met shyly asked, lost and hesitant, whether they were for or against the death penalty. Although the death penalty is entrenched in society and supported by institutions, it is nevertheless an increasingly sensitive subject, still relatively little debated, which divides the population into two unequal parts. On the one hand, there are the activist abolitionists, extremely organized and energetic, but not very representative in numbers, combined with the passive abolitionists, who are ultimately rather indifferent to the cause. On the other, retentionists represent 65% of the population[16], a small proportion of whom are also activists. Nevertheless, the debate is progressing. David Atwood, founder of the Texas Coalition to Abolish the Death Penalty, puts it this way: "The abolitionist movement is new. Our goal is to educate the citizens of our state. We've noticed that when people know a little more about the death penalty, they no longer support it. It's frustrating that things aren't moving faster, but we think things are moving in the right direction."

In Utah, there's a custom of minting a coin for each execution. Transformed into a medal, it represents a trophy symbolizing an act of power and bravery in the service of society. This ceremonial attests to the permeability of American society to the execution of death. There is a desire to perpetuate the event, to make it a collective sacrifice that is deeply rooted in the cultural landscape. However, it would be wrong to claim that the benefits of capital punishment are shared by all. The pride of this trophy is also overshadowed by personal consciences when faced with the death of a man, in the face of a collective conscience that is no longer so unanimous. Regardless of the raw opinion expressed at a distance from the sentence, it must be

16. According to the latest Gallup Poll of October 2009 in response to the question "Do you support the death penalty for someone who has been convicted of murder?"

admitted that there is also an often modest but perceptible discomfort in the execution of a human being. "I don't really find it sad, but it's impossible to rejoice in the death of another man," says Barb Kirk, who came to witness the execution of her father's killer. No one can ignore the fact that the death penalty does not meet with general approval, that the abolitionist movement has emerged over the last fifteen years or so, that there are protest movements at every execution, certainly against the conservative attraction of elected officials, certain preachers with a mercantile and political spirituality, or the media feeding on the "beast" of a sensationalism that must constantly be regenerated as it weakens. There are also public stances taken by personalities, dissident artistic expressions, and readings of the Bible less favorable to institutionalized violence, which sow contradictory glimpses into this skilfully maintained atmosphere of historical retentionism. Even if, as David Atwood points out: "Some churches find it hard to preach abolition, because they know that many of their faithful are for it, and that it's a controversial subject." Although not in the majority, for several decades the Catholic Church has affirmed its condemnation of the death penalty in the United States. However, defenders of the right to life do not appear to be liberals, since they are frequently the same people who will be found in the public arena denouncing abortion as part of the *pro-life* movement, as in the case of this retired woman we met at the Prison Museum in Huntsville, Texas: "I'm pro-life. But I'm also a person who believes we should have laws. I know our laws in America are based on the Holy Bible, which says, 'Thou shalt not kill,' but God also said, 'If you kill a man, you will be killed.'" Another example is the preaching of Jay Gross, pastor of the Southern Baptist Church in Conroe, Texas, when he justifies the death penalty on the basis of the Bible and, at the same time, condemns abortion, arguing that "we've never seen a criminal baby come out of its mother's womb". It should be noted that this church, very powerful in the South, is one of the most pro-death penalty. David Atwood points out that "this may also be why the majority of executions take place in the South, as they base their faith mainly on the Old Testament", which is known to be more violent and severe than the evangelicals' contribution to the new.

This subdivision of opinions reinforces the divide between the American and European models in terms of the evolution of social ideas and political conceptions. Remember, for example, that despite the cost of the death penalty against a backdrop of economic crisis, and despite the 704 condemned prisoners waiting[17] on death row in San Quentin or Chowchilla, California is still not on the road to abolition. Faced with this astronomical figure, Robert R. Bryan, a lawyer specializing in the defense of death row inmates, observes that "the system is self-destructing, collapsing in on itself". This liberal state, governed by the Republicans until January 2011, is also close to legalizing cannabis and gay marriage. We must therefore be vigilant when observing the ideological and cultural subdivisions that reign in the United States. As in many countries, the division of ideas between progressives and conservatives is based on different historical arrangements, shaping the contours of social and political debate according to rules specific to the country concerned. In this sense, the United States may come as a surprise, and abolitionist arguments, just as much as the strategies developed at international level, must necessarily adapt to the specificities of this large, recent country, which is increasingly mixed in cultural terms.

Kill the guilty - spare the innocent

The fantasy of incontrovertibly proven guilt, combined with the fantasy of potentially infallible justice, is declined and argued. "I believe in the death penalty when we're sure we've judged the real culprit," says this Texas citizen. According to this widespread opinion, killing in the name of justice is not in itself reprehensible, as long as innocent people are not executed. This is how the justification for the death penalty is

---

17. As of June 10, 2011, Death Penalty Information Center.

developed, reduced to cases of certain guilt[18], i.e. "confirmable guilt" ideally confirmed by three witnesses[19]. This description of justice is completely detached from the principles of reality that govern crimes and the unprecedented circumstances in which they are committed. Nobody knows how to find witnesses, whether there are always witnesses in any criminal case, whether witnesses can be corrupted, and so on. Ideally, then, all that's needed is a murder, a guilty party and three people who can testify to the guilt of the crime, and the death penalty can be imposed. Such rhetoric has no other purpose than to persist in legitimizing capital punishment while ruling out the possibility of executing the innocent. They suffer from a lack of realism, and are applied within the framework of a scenario elaborated as fiction, disregarding the inherent singularity of each crime. It's worth noting, however, the recurrent concern of pro-death penalty advocates to see a punishment applied wisely. In people's minds, this is the price to pay for capital punishment to retain all its credibility and therefore its deterrent virtues. The punishment of the most terrible crimes must not be turned into a crime by the execution of an innocent person. There is therefore a moral idea behind the defense of the death penalty, almost of the order of wisdom. "Who will he kill again if we let him live?" asks Barb Kirk, who has come to witness the execution of her father's killer. The abolitionists' discourse cannot ignore this dimension. Capital punishment is not defended as a barbarity to be used in excess, but as a punishment to be meted out without appeal to those who can be determined, supposedly infallibly, to be the perpetrators of atrocities. In this case, and only in this case, executing a guilty party is nothing more than the definitive elimination of an individual who has chosen not to deserve to live. Debra Saunders, a journalist

---

18. The Talmud proscribed the death penalty on the grounds of the ontological impossibility of certainty.

19. This figure is repeatedly put forward, without any rational explanation. The number 3, unbreakable by half, seems to be a guarantee of seriousness. In fact, it is always more impersonal than the number 2, which refers to a couple possibly united by a common purpose. The number 1, on the other hand, is too prone to partiality.

with the *San Francisco Chronicle*, defends the death penalty in this way: "When I think of the Libyan who was sentenced in Scotland to 27 years in prison and then released after 9 years, even though he was responsible for the deaths of 270 people by blowing up a plane, is that fair? It's an American argument that doesn't speak to Europe, but when the crime is so terrible, it must be punished proportionately, in this case with the death penalty." Nevertheless, there are many who are willing to work around this drawback, as evidenced by the speech of Jay Gross, preacher at the Southern Baptist Church in Conroe, Texas: "If we no longer execute for fear of killing an innocent person, then we should also open the prison doors, because we can be sure that there are innocent people inside." He ends his preaching by declaring: "We are a great nation and we have never been afraid to do our duty, even when innocent people were going to suffer. When we bombed France to liberate Europe from the Nazi yoke, of course innocent people died. But it had to be done, and we're proud to have done it. It's the same with the death penalty!" This is how capital punishment continues to be legitimized in the United States, despite the cases of innocence that regularly mar the application of a justice system that some would like to see beyond reproach.

The invisible hand of the powerful

The institution of justice is frequently perceived by death row inmates and their entourage as dictated by the interests of the powerful, who are in practice exempt from any capital punishment, and whose power depends on the social submission of the masses. These powerful people are both often cited and very imprecisely described by death row inmates during interviews. Those who ultimately pull the strings that lock up the poorest, or worse, put them to death, are defined as the chosen and the possessors, the barely-identified "few" who have the power to decide for the many. A death row inmate from San Quentin, California, refers to them indefinitely as "them", "they", pointing to the cities of San Francisco and Sacramento in the distance. These are the decision-makers in their luxurious offices, those with chauffeurs and rich villas, those whose caricatured security discourse is publicized by the media. Only these voices carry weight and influence, based on what the majority want to hear, i.e., an often populist vision, using demagoguery to ensure the ease of re-election to the posts of governor, state judge, district attorney or sheriff. It's not a question of skin color, even if this group is indeed composed more of *"White Americans"*. It's the feeling of a form of domination of the masses for the benefit of concentrated power and wealth, expressed by the hand of the judge, the pen of the prosecution, and a judicial clockwork sufficiently imprecise to leave the field open to numerous "little arrangements with the law" often qualified as corruption. E. M., sentenced to death in Parchman, Mississippi, puts it into perspective: "I'm not afraid of the others here, if not of the Court and the judges, they're the most dangerous for us here. I'm afraid of the justice system in general. They have the power to do whatever they want, it's power more than justice, they're the most powerful." This Austin court reporter[20] explains, "On the outside, people have faith in the system, because they think convicts have plenty of opportunities to prove their innocence. In reality, the system doesn't work like that. The state has a lot of money, but the defense has much less. Death row inmates are mostly poor, less-educated and from minority backgrounds. And they can't afford the lawyers they need to counter the power of the prosecution. The balance of power is skewed in favor of the state and against the poor." This justifies the feeling of exclusion on the part of those condemned to death, similar to that of many prisoners in the jails of other nations. Everywhere, the justice system is said to operate at different speeds, depending on whether it concerns rich decision-makers or poor citizens. However, it should be noted that this assessment takes on another dimension when it comes to an irreversible sentence involving the vital process in the context of the exercise of an authority that appears intransigent. What's more, in contrast to recruitment based on merit and academic achievement, the elective process for state judges, district attorneys and sheriffs is

---

20. Jordan SMITH, *Austin Chronicle* journalist, interview conducted in June 2010.

experienced by death row inmates as an exclusion of anyone without the financial means to engage in costly election campaigns. As a result, despite the presence of jurors representing society in criminal trials, justice is perceived as an institution jealously guarded in the hands of those with a personal interest in making it work. As the father of a death row inmate puts it: "When you start getting caught up in a court case, even on spurious grounds, it's very hard to get out!" He adds: "When they've been elected (state judges and District Attorneys), they all want to be re-elected, so they convict more and more people. They don't care if they're guilty or innocent, they just need to convict and then execute!" In judicial matters, the system is described as an inequitable oligarchy, whose power supplants the right to a quality defense, like a trap closing on the lives of a not inconsiderable number of citizens, admittedly generally guilty, even dangerous, who identify themselves as the victims of an implacable and unjust mechanism. In this sense, the desire for democratic justice based on the judgment of peers, while ambitious in theory, reveals here and there often culpable and prejudicial imperfections.

Killing to save taxes: the value of illegitimate lives

This argument, as surprising as it may seem, not only in its construction, but above all in the ease with which it is expressed, is a widespread thought, shared by the greatest number of people. Here too, it's through ignorance of a reality that is nevertheless objectivized by figures, that everyone considers capital punishment to be a more favorable cost-saving measure than life imprisonment. From an accounting point of view, let's remember that the cost of a capital sentence, taking into account the price of specific trials and investigative processes to counter the irreversible aspect of the sentence, is around three to five times more expensive than a prison sentence, even a life sentence, i.e. several million dollars versus around 600,000 for a prison sentence in a criminal trial. For the average person, the only thing on their mind is the daily cost of prison: $47 on average. For him, it's better to execute than to have to feed, care for, heat and lock up people. Like many of the opinions expressed, a retired woman from Texas explains, Bible in hand: "Oh no, I'm against life sentences! So we can pay with our taxes? As a taxpayer, I think they should be executed as soon as they're found guilty. But that's never quick here, they wait for years and sometimes die in prison before being executed[21]! I think that despite the fact that perhaps sometimes innocent people have been executed, we need our system. I have to look at the fact that we pay for them. And then also the fact that there are still a lot of criminals loose on the streets!" Others explain, "As a taxpayer, I don't want to pay for the comfort of criminals, I'd rather know they're dead."

Here again, it would be difficult to know where the figures come from, but they often suggest that 30 days after the trial would be a reasonable time to wait before carrying out the execution: "As soon as we know they're guilty, we have to carry out the sentence, by any means, hanging, injection, shooting, electrocution" says Jo, a retiree from Texas, and "there's no reason to wait, a guilty man is a guilty man!" What about the remedies that are indispensable in a democratic society? What about the right of the defense to have the validity of the sentence and due process reviewed by other judges? What about lying witnesses, corrupt judges, District Attorneys, police and prosecutors? What about the media's relentless pursuit of the case? What about the political stakes and personal careers that seem to frequently inspire the workings of the judiciary? What about the fallibility of any human system? Everyone is driven by the idea that things are simple, that good justice is swift justice, that as soon as the police have found a suspect, as soon as a narrative makes it possible to determine the causality linking an individual to a crime, then the person must be found guilty and executed. Why wait any longer, why spend money on appeals and expert reports, why keep them alive in prison? It's easy to see things in simplistic, binary, Manichean terms. Besides, executing a

---

21. In California, for example, since executions resumed in 1976, 13 death row inmates have been executed, 52 have died of natural causes, and 18 death row inmates have committed suicide.

criminal is not the same as killing a human being. As Rick Halperin, professor of human rights at Southern Methodist University in Dallas, Texas, points out, death row inmates are considered "garbage, vermin, subhuman, trash" for whom all compassion is useless and all expense is a waste of money. Curtis McCarty, exonerated after 22 years of incarceration, recalls his arrival on death row: "The guys incarcerated were nothing like the monsters I expected. My parents realized that too, that everything is done to encourage people to hate us. Hate us, abuse us, then kill us…"

Humans are no longer human when they are reduced to a costly entity. Killing those who are denied the status of *fellow human beings*, and therefore the right to life, in order to limit public spending: this opinion, widely held in retentionist states of all generations, gives an idea of how death row inmates are viewed by society on the outside. Kevin Cooper, an inmate in San Quentin, California, realizes: "We're seen as submerged, despised and forgotten. People don't even know we're here anymore. And no one ever imagines that there are innocent people here. Nobody has a critical view of the system. People believe in justice as a fair system that works. It reassures them. We're the bad guys. But what right do they have to kill us Blacks, the poor? They own us like we used to own slaves. It's torture! […] I didn't know anything about it myself. It didn't interest me before." This rejection of those condemned to death is without appeal, without indulgence; it obeys the binarity of reasoning that is clearly not very well-developed from the moment it takes into account only one dimension, that of the facts reproached, to sum up the complexity of the human personality. "Before I was confronted with my son's death sentence, I thought with this severity," says a mother in Texas. This specificity in the United States stems from the fact that all aspects of existence are, at one time or another, represented under the parameter of cost or gain, two notions representing the main signifier, both in thought and discourse. It's a cultural language we have to come to terms with when working for abolition in the United States. This is why the revelation of the reality of the cost of death penalty trials, involving lengthy investigations, is an argument increasingly developed by abolitionists on the other side of the Atlantic.

When you want to kill your dog, you say it has rabies

One of the arguments put forward by retentionists is that execution prevents death row inmates from continuing to kill their counterparts or guards, either on the outside or on death row. This idea is based on the fact that, with nothing left to lose, individuals banished from society would feel no impediment to embodying the indelible image projected onto them, i.e. criminals, sub-humans to be slaughtered, animals without consideration or emotion. Once rejected from the human community, these individuals would only wish to continue killing their fellow human beings like bloodthirsty beasts. In the United States, this concept is based on the idea that the human community's obedience to regulations can only be sustained by the public and implicit recognition of belonging to a society imagined as a homogeneous entity, expressed forcefully in July 4th ceremonies behind the phrase "We, the American people". Yet, contrary to this vision, in "maximum security" prisons, contact between inmates on death row provides few opportunities to attempt this kind of violence. Similarly, the official restriction on possession of weapons in detention makes it difficult to use them unless there is an illicit trade with warders. Given the conditions of isolation in cages, and the regular shackling of hands and feet on every move, it is hard to imagine these killings continuing. However, as with all systems of punitive confinement, death rows are also sometimes jungles in which survival is not always easy. Curtis McCarty, a former death row inmate from McAlester, Oklahoma, recalls: "You just have to be stronger and assert yourself in an 'I'll kill you' tone. Still, there are guilty and violent people on death row. And a lot of people are killed in prison, especially with homemade knives. We used to make chest protectors out of National Geographic, like homemade bulletproofs. It's another crazy planet, with racism, poverty and mental illness. To survive, you have to belong to a group, a gang, it can be a non-gang, i.e.

Chapter 3: Cultural and Societal Portrait of a Young Country

a group that rejects gangs, so it's a gang too. I was authoritarian. Gangs made life impossible between inmates and guards. That's why we made our own gang with friends, with people who have since been killed in bad circumstances." In Pennsylvania, Mumia Abu-Jamal, incarcerated for 29 years on death row, adds: "There is sometimes violence between inmates, who try to fight over plastic trays, for example. But most gangs disappeared from Philadelphia in the sixties and seventies. In fact, there are very few left in Pittsburgh."

These rumors of unmanageable violence behind the thick concrete walls of death row also constitute, for the population outside, a denial of the individual's capacity to change. In practice, depending on how it's managed, confinement and general deprivation don't turn everyone into indomitable beasts. Indeed, Ricky Bell, the warden of Nashville's Riverbend prison, confides, "The population on death row is renowned for being easy to monitor." The worst criminals, weaned on their outer demons, often soften. This notion of locked-up wild beasts is conveyed without any foundation other than the emergence of behaviors as violent as they are exceptional, generalized to excess. It serves to sweep aside at a stroke the inescapable question of who these people whom justice wants to kill have become.

The register of faith and irrationality

In everyone's lexical field, words don't spontaneously mislead intentions, but carry within them a confession of thoughts and feelings. When asked about the death penalty, the most common expression is: *I believe in the death penalty, I believe in our justice system.*[22] This principled adherence, governed by an approach similar to the irrationality of religious faiths, excludes any critical vision of the death penalty and justice. If the laws are the way they are, it's because the government has designed them to meet society's imperatives. Penalties and the judicial and police systems belong to an untouchable domain,

---

22. "I believe in the death penalty and I have faith in our justice system."

like a blindly defended caste. The only way to have access to a critical dimension is to be concerned in one's flesh or affect by a more concrete principle of reality revealing the faces of justice. After defending a death row inmate as part of a *pro bono* defense[23], this lawyer from a major business law firm confides: "I thought that criminal justice operated according to the same rules of fairness as civil trials. In fact, I realized the inequity between the prosecution and the defense when I took on Michael's case. The prosecutor knew more than I did, and had the right to withhold evidence. It's difficult in this case to fight on equal terms." James G. Rytting, a public defender in Houston, explains: "On a regular basis, the prosecution allows itself to make huge mistakes and malfunctions, and that's when we, the defense, have to bring in evidence to restore justice. But in practice, we can't be satisfied with minor errors; on the contrary, we have to highlight enormous ineptitudes, which exist most of the time, but which the prosecution has taken care to disguise! [...] In the case of my client, Mr. Green, the prosecution's expert was chosen to lie and deny the facts. He explains the "Machiavellianism that was put in place": "The State was not going to give Mr. Green a stay of execution, because this was the rape and murder of a 12-year-old girl, and a white one at that. So everything was clear and decided in advance between the District Attorney and the judge."[24]

Criticizing this faith in the system also presupposes having the intellectual tools to free oneself from faithful, unconditional adherence to the nation's structure. As this university professor in Dallas, Texas, explains: "In my country, it's easy to be considered a traitor if you criticize its institutions." The endorsement of the death penalty in

---

23. *Pro bono* defense, i.e. where the costs are borne by an outside entity. This is a form of "contractual" generosity in which corporate bodies or individuals, *through* their own law firms, assume responsibility for the defense of an indigent defendant.

24. In the event, G. was granted a stay of execution by another judge on the Texas Court of Criminal Justice Appeals, who seems to have discovered the many ineptitudes of his colleagues. To date, at the end of 2010, G. has not been executed.

the United States stems from this faith in the *system* considered, not without arrogance and credulity, to be the "*best system in the* world"[25]. It's a faith that reassures, and an almost structural inability to criticize the foundations and specificities of American society and the political-judicial system that governs it. All this rhetoric seems far removed from justice, and is more akin, for death row inmates and their loved ones, to the expression of a sense of injustice that is silenced by prison walls, so as to render impervious the society outside, which can then drape itself in its deafness and blindness. Hence, no doubt, the lack of critical vision of a penal system in which people claim to believe as one believes in God. To have faith is also to have doubt, but not to express it. Steve Hall of the StandDown Texas Project adds: "Why are all the arguments against the death penalty, but nobody knows? It's a matter of education to teach people to conclude from the facts. The problem is that people have deep-seated beliefs that don't lead them to look at the facts, which are very resistant to reality." This believer we met in Texas corroborates, Bible in hand, by acknowledging, without any inflection, what others frequently express: "If one of my relatives, my husband or my child, had committed a crime, I also think he should be executed! I wouldn't have a problem with that. I just want the law to be applied, that's all!"

American time: the benefits and drawbacks of a short-term view

Penalties in the United States are also governed by a particular conception of time that governs the whole of American society. Compared to the vast majority of countries on the planet, American society as it is constituted today is a cultural amalgam that has only recently been organized. It's a young society, made up of multiple imports that have come to make up a country, a nation in perpetual motion, with no ancestral roots to regulate it. The past is always relative, like time itself. By comparison with so many other places, we have to admit that a society with such vitality and such a short, little-shared common

---

25. "Best system in the world".

past cannot live on the achievements of the diffuse shadow it leaves in its wake. Because the foundations of the past are little-known and relatively recent, initiatives and thoughts are more focused on the present and the near future, than on shared, centuries-old experience. This parameter represents the genius of a society with adolescent energy, capable of rebirth and adaptation like no other. It is also the aporia that encloses and prevents a form of wisdom, in this case that of recognizing that, guilty or innocent, the lives of others are in some way one's own, and that the aim of a society is to appease intrinsic violence by fighting against all the mechanisms that promote it. This is the visual and conceptual field of American society, assimilated to a low horizon and articulated on an approach governed by short times. The imperative always consists in satisfying a need belonging to the present or the near future, taking into account the impact of this behavior only in the short term. This way of thinking gives rise to a continual ability to bounce back, innovate, adapt and renew. Even if it proves imprecise, this field of vision knows few obstacles. It provides motivation and energy for some, while leaving others stranded, unable to keep up with a frantic succession that never considers the day after tomorrow. It authorizes the radicality of death as a supposedly immediate response to the crimes committed. Those excluded from this relentless movement are in ghettos, in prison, or worse, on death row. They also have loved ones, children and spouses whom society, blinded by the need for radical punishment, refuses to recognize. Their pain and the resulting consequences already belong to the day after tomorrow, a day we don't know today and will define differently tomorrow. As soon as the death sentence is pronounced, the situation of the condemned is quickly forgotten by the outside world, already drawn by the emotions of other events.

The ambivalent freedom of a chosen people

The word has become a slogan, which by dint of being repeated like a mantra, ends up reaching the most tenuous of consciences. Freedom is conceived as a good, a bulwark against evil, and the hypnotic capabilities of the word often tend to extinguish, or worse, render immoral any form of criticism. During a preaching session in Conroe, Texas, Jay Gross explains to the congregation: "Our great country is founded on freedom, a freedom that all envy us and that we must defend, even with arms. We are free because of our laws, our Constitution, whose terms are inspired by God from the Bible. That is our strength!" Since the death penalty takes place in THE land of freedoms, and since laws are often recognized as being divinely inspired, there's nothing wrong with that. He adds: "The people who practice injections must understand that they are ministers of the state, like governors, like combatants during war, they are instruments of God, therefore, and of the government."

Journalists, meanwhile, claim to be free to write for or against the death penalty. In this sense, the United States stands apart from authoritarian regimes. Yet, in a way, the construction of American society, behind the symbols and all the forms of representation that govern it, is subject to a kind of "brainwashing" that annihilates all resistance and reduces the debate of ideas to a sometimes murderous indifference. Behind the numbing of the word "*freedom*" lies a more despicable reality, unknown to the general public with its amnesiac conscience. This former death row inmate from Oklahoma is not fooled by the latitude given to abolitionist activism: "Mrs. D. can speak out against the death penalty as she likes, because she's a notable person, she has money and consideration. But for others, the police seek to intimidate them because they go against the system; they may, for example, have problems at airports, including being intimidated on internal flights." On the other hand, paradoxically, the land of the free represents at the same time 5% of the world's population and 23.4% of the world's prison population[26]. Up close, the conditions

---

26. "According to the summary [...] the USA incarcerates 23.4% of the world's prison population. In this report, the total for the USA as at December 31, 2007 [see p. 3] does not include juveniles", WALMSLEY (Roy), *International Center for Prison Suicides*, London, King's College Law School, 2009.

of confinement in American prisons are driven solely by the need for security, while denying dignity. As David Atwood points out: "Solitary confinement can drive you mad. It's psychologically disastrous, and that should change. The treatment they receive should be more humane. He adds: "It's a very difficult existence, some cope better than others. Many try to commit suicide." This observation, in stark contrast to the idealized image of a dream country, is impossible for the vast majority of Americans to accept.

In reality, the freedom they talk about is more that of making money, and being able to spend it, at any time of the day or night: "For these reasons, for entrepreneurship, for choosing one's life, the United States is a fantastic country," says Rick Halperin, a university professor in Dallas, Texas. But what about the freedom to come and go without the risk of being mugged? For a woman, freedom also means being able to walk down the street at night without the risk of being mugged by armed men. And therein lies the uniqueness of this gigantic country, always fascinating for better or worse, but also frightening at times. Rick Halperin ironizes: "Just because you wear an America pin doesn't mean you're free. If you live in fear of violence, that's not freedom. He adds: "It's an easy country, it's a consumerist society, you can buy what you want, choose where to live, and choose what you want. We associate that with freedom, and that's one form of it. But there's another form of freedom: the freedom of fear, the freedom of knowing that everyone else is as free as we are. It's a false freedom, a society intolerant of the freedom of other countries, of social justice, of human dignity…"

Commemorations of the country's greatness, of the validity of its choices throughout recent or ancient history, of the near-perfection of its institutions, feed the drowsiness of consciences and inhibit their critical sense, sometimes with the support of religion, which spreads the representation of a censorious and inspiring god, as witnessed by the unfolding of this Sunday service in a Southern Baptist church in

Texas, with these words: "*The only hope for America is God* [...] *There is no one like OUR God* [...]"[27]; or these quotes from the preaching: "God gives the mission to governments to organize executions and the death penalty", relying on this biblical reality: "Jesus is the best known of those condemned to death, he lived the death penalty for us, this is the foundation of our faith [...]".

Criticism of the death penalty in the United States comes up against the arrogance of a country whose population remains convinced, whatever its recurrent historical drifts, that the American "*Way of Life*"[28] is the best and most enviable. Everyone is certain that this new country has been built up efficiently and thoughtfully, without the burden of cultural heritages, and with the ability to avoid repeating the counter-productive mistakes of the Old World in the New World. It's striking to note, not only in the newspapers and on television, but also in conversation at the drop of a hat, how ignorant Americans are of the rest of the world. "You don't have the death penalty in Europe? But how do you punish criminals?" they ask. Over and above a constructed culture, this undeniable phenomenon is fraught with meaning. It is also undoubtedly due to the history of a recent society formed by the amalgamation of individuals of diverse origins who, in order to begin this new life in a hoped-for El Dorado, forget their own respective roots to melt into a system whose workings they accept from the moment their presence on the territory is precisely the result of this fierce will to live and survive characteristic of the immigrants they themselves are or who preceded them. This cab driver, who immigrated to California over 30 years ago, remembers his native Great Britain: "Over there, I know that we no longer have the death penalty; we consider that the State has no right to take people's lives. It's true that here, when aggression happens to us, then we have a different

---

27. "God is America's only hope. Nothing beats our God."

28. Lifestyle. This is a particularly developed and recurrent notion in the United States, signifying the specificity of a population in its approach to essentials, satisfactions, successes, but also prohibitions.

point of view." And in these circumstances, when the here is so vast, so incorporating by a pervasive culture, the elsewhere is forgotten, disappears, becomes inconsistent to the point of never being either inspiring or prescriptive.

In the United States, people are against torture, incredulously rejecting the idea that their country could be the perpetrator. At the very least, this was the general opinion before the population recognized the imperative need to fight terrorism following the events of September 11, 2001. The population deplores genocide and behaves like a civilized society, using the same criteria and parameters as any Western country. And yet, in the 21st century, society is still struggling to take a critical view of capital punishment. What happens abroad has no influence in the United States. What's more, the foreigner is a vague, uniform notion, supposed to speak the same language, whose geographical location remains uncertain. Cultural exchanges are a one-way street. Throughout the world, the United States prescribes a large number of practices, consumption habits, ideas and lifestyles. And yet, this great country, no doubt because of its size and multitude, remains relatively impervious to external developments. Jay Gross explains in his Sunday sermon: "Other countries want to tell us how to behave, especially on the question of justice. But we know that our system is good, that it is just, that our laws are inspired by the Bible, that's what's important. Should we listen to their criticism of us? No, we shouldn't! Our choices are the right ones, and no one should tell us how to behave. We've built ourselves on this freedom, and that's our success." This is commonly referred to as arrogance, which, while not wrong, is inaccurate. It's true that the United States is a recent nation of *self-made men*, accountable only to themselves. The result is a self-centeredness that makes 300 million people amnesic to the fact that there are 200 other countries in the world, each with their own issues, some of which run counter to American points of view. There is also a tendency to maintain a sense of sovereignty. The American myth hangs on its illusions of influence and success, as the unprecedented model of a successful society, made up of the ideal combination of the varied contributions of each immigrant, weighted down by the imperfections of the Old Continent. Never mind the differences that exist elsewhere, never mind disregarding what might inspire in a beneficial way. American pride means reinventing everything on a national level, sifting every subject by the yardstick of internal culture with a contempt that generates indifference and ignorance about the outside world. This cultural choice gives rise to excesses and energies of perpetual renewal, but also to a form of inertia in the face of the imperative need for self-criticism. This state of affairs must be taken into account when it comes to expecting effects from the international movement in favor of universal abolition. Respectively, the ideas of "international" and "universal" do not generate the expected effects, as if it were difficult, if not impossible, to increment an evolutionary process on the New Continent. We need to understand that, in addition to political sovereignty, there is also cultural, popular and social sovereignty, which acts as a hermetic bulwark against the civilizational thrusts that can be identified elsewhere. Although general, there are a few caveats to this observation. David Atwood tempers this reality a little: "The worldwide abolitionist movement helps us, because even if people say 'we don't care what people say elsewhere', in fact there are many citizens here for whom it matters. If we can show that the U.S. is isolating itself, these people will wake up and say 'why are we doing this when everyone else is going in the opposite direction?' We talk about this in debates. We point to Europe as an example, saying that we're one of the last industrialized countries that still has the death penalty. We're proving by all means how isolated we are."

The American abolitionist movement makes no mistake when it develops pragmatic arguments that can be heard by a large number of people, in contrast to the moral debates that led to abolition in other countries. Take, for example, the popular and cultural impetus of the Journey of Hope[29], an association of families of homicide victims founded by Bill Pelke, and joined by families of death row inmates, families of executed inmates, the innocent and others who have experiences to share, notably through public educational interventions to discuss solutions that avoid recourse to the death penalty. Through the power of testimonies divulged throughout the United States, this movement responds to the many ignorances and questions of a population attached to the death penalty as an inescapable penal concept. There is also the promotion of strategies aimed at progressively reducing capital crimes, regularly bringing out numerical studies that challenge the rationality of retentionist arguments. These are all progressive maneuvers consciously adapted by abolitionists to combat the blocks of certainties and tamed practices that govern the inertia of American society.

A binary society: good guys and bad guys

When it comes to criminal justice, the nation itself is divided into two blocs: abolitionist states, some of which have been abolitionist for over a century[30], and states that persist in using the death penalty. Often, the most vociferous supporters of the death penalty are white-skinned individuals[31], financially well off enough to be among those who own and consume. Ownership determines the contours of the need for protection. Society is also divided between those who believe in a god who punishes and those who believe in a god who forgives, for whom the redemption of faults takes place in the afterlife, after death. This gave rise to a range of different preaching practices, all aimed at enlisting a particular category of faithful, with success measured

---

29. Journey of Hope… From Violence to Healing, an association of victims' families, founded by Bill Pelke in 1993.

30. Michigan abolished it in 1846, Maine in 1887, Wisconsin in 1853, and Minnesota in 1911.

31. See, in particular, a poll conducted in Maryland: "Whites are far more supportive of the death penalty than blacks (70% to 43%), and more men than women support the death penalty (66% to 54%)", WAGNER (John) and AGIESTA (Jennifer), "Voters remain divided on the death penalty", *Washington Post*, May 11, 2010.

by the number of people who flocked to their churches. In the heart of the countryside, in Oklahoma or elsewhere, opinions in favor of executions are thus expressed in colloquial fashion: *"Kill them all!"* or *"Fry the bastard!"*[32] At this level, the encounter with the American population sometimes smacks of barbarism. These radical positions are reminiscent of the binary vision of the world, society and individuals most accessible to the human brain, which aims to distinguish between the good guys and the bad guys, those whose behavior is acceptable and those who are definitively degraded. The latter do not deserve to retain the prerogatives attributed to human beings. Execution therefore corresponds to the paroxysmal suppression of their rights. The right to life demonstrates that, as a right, it is not de facto immutable. There is a need for education to counter this idea. "If I kill someone, all I expect is to be judged and executed," says this retiree in Texas, who adds, "If it was my son or daughter on death row, I wouldn't mind. I'd tell them 'kill them'. That's how I feel… Don't count on me to go visit them. They've done something wrong, that's their problem, let them pay!" Far from being an exception, this radical approach confirms that capital punishment is applied in all circumstances, in response to behavior identified as criminal, irrespective of any other assessment that might be mitigated. Regardless of whether it's your own flesh and blood, to be the perpetrator of a crime is to be sure of the corresponding punishment, to be radically on the side of the evil to be fought without any weakness, not even the indulgence of a mother or a spouse. There's no point in wavering; justice through law must always be the strongest, and above all never give in to the weakness of emotion and affect.

Abolitionist activists in the U.S. have noted that retentionist opinions are closely linked to ignorance. And yet, we civilize ourselves by qualifying actions, facts, matter and feelings. What is a crime? What are the facts

---

32. "We've got to kill them all!" or "Let's fry the bastards!" Far from being anecdotal responses, these phrases are expressed shamelessly by the American population, particularly in the context of this survey work conducted among the general public to obtain general opinions on capital punishment.

and who are the protagonists? What is prison like? What does it really mean to execute? In these conditions where knowledge is not acquired, symbolism and beliefs take up too much room, leading to an irrefutable and taboo faith in the taste for blood, perceived as a weapon of justice. Sister Helen Prejean, author of *The Last March*[33], describes support for the death penalty in the USA as "a mile wide, but an inch deep". She wants to make it clear that retentionists appear numerous, but in reality, their will is not strong enough to resist the power of awareness of what the death penalty is once you get close to it. In her view, anyone who confronts the issue of the death penalty more closely inevitably becomes critical of this violent and unjust device. From a distance, there are only two reassuring colors that rule out doubt and discussion. Up close, the Manichean vision is suddenly no longer satisfactory.

The binary vision means that individuals are viewed without relief. In order to obtain a death sentence, it is also necessary to reduce an individual to his actions, to summarize his existence in a single chapter of his story. All the rest of the individual's personality and background is then viewed in the light of this first conviction. This is the role of the criminal trial, which must be constructed to ensure that the 12 jurors vote unanimously in favor of the death penalty. It's enough to blacken what is already gray, to consider that whiteness is lost forever, and that with the crime committed, it is human identity that is lost. Forever. In reality, which people do their best not to touch, there is a parallel world between all these individual experiences, which are never mentioned, for fear of compassion, understanding or forgiving the traits that are harshly portrayed publicly or privately to justify the need to kill in the name of justice. Yet the behavior observed among death row inmates during confinement attests to changes. Those who had killed under the influence of psychotropic substances were weaned off alcohol and

---

33. PREJEAN (Sister Helen), *Dead Man Walking: An Eyewitness Account of the Death Penalty in the United States*, New York, Vintage Books, A division of Random House Inc., 1994. Adapted for the screen by Tim Robbins, with Susan Sarandon and Sean Penn in the lead roles.

Chapter 3: Cultural and Societal Portrait of a Young Country

drugs during their years in detention. Imposed asceticism, combined with maturity and reading for some, led to reflection and changes in personal options over the years, particularly for those who were not mentally unbalanced[34]. The anathema cast by society *via* the institution of justice in matters of the death penalty therefore appears to be pointless severity, disconnected from a more factual reading of destinies. The reality of life shows that colors are never so marked and indelible. Black and white become a multitude of grays in which everyone can find themselves, contrary to the implacable judgment for which society had vowed reassuring permanence. Whatever they may have committed 10 or 20 years ago, it often seems difficult to see death row inmates as the embodiment of any danger to society. What can we say about Mumia Abu-Jamal, locked up for 29 years, author of numerous books and articles on American society: who can claim that his execution will make American society better and more serene? What can we say about Caryl Chessman[35] and the many anonymous men and women executed to satisfy a sentence for a crime committed, but also in defiance of real, profound changes in their lives? What can we say about Stanley Tookie Williams[36], founder of the Crips gang on the outside, then anti-gang

---

34. Death rows and prisons in the U.S. are, as everywhere else in the world, populated by desocialized individuals, disobedient to the law, often for reasons of mental health. The U.S. Supreme Court forbids executing anyone who does not have an enlightened understanding of the meaning of the sentence. For the rest, in the United States as elsewhere, the question arises of confining to prison a population that requires care rather than punishment. Clearly, in many of these cases, prison appears to be a resignation on the part of society, which prefers to set people aside rather than face up to the costs and structure required upstream, to resolve social problems, and downstream, to treat their mental health. Since providing care is not the same as punishing, popular vengeance cannot be satisfied with this solidarity-based approach, which requires paying taxes to provide care.

35. Caryl Chessman was executed on May 2, 1960 by asphyxiation in the gas chamber of San Quentin prison, California. He is the author of several books written on death row, notably on the death penalty in the United States: *Cell 2455* Death *Row*, 1954; *Trial by Ordeal*, 1955; *The Face of* Justice, 1957; *The Kid Was a Killer*, 1960.

36. Sentenced to death for murder and executed on December 13, 2005 at San Quentin penitentiary, California. However, this living figure of rehabilitation was not pardoned by Governor Schwarzenegger. His execution by lethal injection was long and painful, and sparked off a major controversy in the United States.

activist on death row? In prison, he learned Latin and sacred texts, then gradually became a recognized campaigner for peace and non-violence. He dedicated his last years to "preventing others from falling here". His children's books have been translated and published all over the world. He was even nominated for the Nobel Peace Prize. It was he who, thanks to an audio recording, succeeded in bringing an end to the violent conflict between the Crips and the Bloods, two Los Angeles gangs. David Powell was executed in Texas on June 15, 2010, for murdering a police officer 32 years earlier. At the time of the execution, an Austin police officer confided, "The man who is going to be put to death for the murder of Ralph Ablanedo is not the man who committed the murder," adding that David Powell had long since become "an old man who has shown what I believe to be true remorse for his crime"[37].

The strange complicity of the media

With a few exceptions, executions remain confined to the alcoves of death chambers, and receive little publicity in the media. Lost in the hustle and bustle of their respective existences, executions are thus lived out in the general indifference of American citizens. For a long time, the subject of the death penalty was rarely broached. There is little public debate on this civilizational cause, as if being in favor of capital punishment were generally accepted, while being an abolitionist constituted an opinion against the current of a system.

In reality, the death penalty only concerns a minority of citizens, a silent minority that produces nothing. As Steve Hall, director of the StandDown Texas Project, explains: "Most people don't think the death penalty will have any impact on them. Only the worst of the worst would ever be affected by the death penalty. That's the idealized version people want to believe in, but it's very far from reality." In fact, unless we're talking about a condemned man who's very well

---

37. "David Powell, model prisoner, to be executed 30 years after his conviction", Le Monde.fr with AFP, June 15, 2010.

known because he gets a lot of media coverage, the media hardly ever announce executions. There's a mixture between the duty to keep informed, indifference, and the awareness of having nothing more to report than an ancient crime, forgotten during these years of appeals, when the news is teeming with freshly spilled blood, crudely portrayed murderers and the recent successes of the judicial process.

On the contrary, the media feed daily on a perverse and sensational trade in criminal cases[38], diluted and detailed, used and abused to keep a population ever more inclined to justify the reality of a continual feeling of fear. In order to instill paranoia in a population of voters expecting "exemplary punishment" from the political powers that be, television, relayed by the press, feeds a daily trade in the criminal affairs that never fail to occur in this great country. Between gore and sensationalism, the narration of the facts takes on a very special importance in the application of capital punishment. Descriptions of the most atrocious crimes in the most horrific circumstances make you want revenge, without hindsight or analysis, as if the reality of the facts were to be treated like a TV series, echoing them for their respective and common benefit. Everything is a possible show: the crime committed, the person executed, the person pardoned. There's no ideology in the treatment of this information, but rather the certainty of being able to convert emotions into economics, which allows the information to exist. Meanwhile, Steven Kreytak, a journalist with *The Austin American-Statesman*, explains that it is his duty to inform his readers with a certain amount of detail, however crude, in order to provide the most accurate information possible in a democratic society. He acknowledges that this transparency of the facts may indeed have a secondary effect on the popular will when it comes to demanding justice. We must also recognize that, conversely,

---

38. Crime in the United States is estimated at 5.4 homicides per 100,000 inhabitants, four times higher than the average for European countries. (*Crime in the United States 2008*, Department of Justice - Federal Bureau of Investigation, USA, September 2009, June 16, 2010). By comparison, France has a rate of 1.35 homicides per 100,000 inhabitants. (Intentional Homicide Rate, UNDATA 2008.)

the scandal-hungry media can be of considerable help in promoting abolitionist campaigns, notably by revealing the great contemporary ineptitudes of capital punishment: the cost of sentencing, the innocent killed, the cost of the innocent, judicial and police dysfunctions, and so on. In this respect, and because cleavages are not immutable, let us cite the recent turnaround of the *Dallas Morning News*, until then a defender of capital punishment in Texas, whose editorials and treatment of court cases have since 2007 revealed an assertive critique of the dangers of the death penalty: "We do not believe that a judicial system, designed by fundamentally fallible human beings, can determine, with moral certainty, the guilt of every defendant convicted of murder."[39]

A gregarious need for blood

By habit or instinct, the population clamors for the death penalty as a need to kill, remaining deaf to consequences and even more so to external judgments. Blood must flow, force must be exerted, indulgence is outlawed: "If you've killed someone, we'll kill you!" say the Americans interviewed in chorus. It's almost like divine punishment, embodied in the power of judges. In a religious America, capital punishment belongs to this level of justification. It is the paroxysmal solution to punishment when it comes to responding to the paroxysm of crime. Because while public opinion sums up its radical position in terms of the law of retaliation, without ever specifying the modalities of application and indulgence, moderate legal actors and connoisseurs demand the application of the death penalty, as provided for by law, to the most terrible crimes. Giving blood when the people are crying out for it - this is the symbolic and concrete function of a system which, in the United States as elsewhere, contains a resurgent sacrificial dimension. As the Mississippi lawyer who witnessed his client's execution summed up: "Unlike watching a grandfather die at 85, watching someone die in these conditions is like some kind of ceremony, something solemn, supernatural, I found it immoral, I was angry, and

---

39. "Death no more", *Dallas Morning News*, April 18, 2007.

Chapter 3: Cultural and Societal Portrait of a Young Country

I understood that I could never again take part in this kind of staging. Nothing can prepare you for this. With the death penalty, atonement is not just for the victim, but also for his or her loved ones, friends on death row who, in Texas for example, see their fellow human beings disappear one by one. E. M., a prisoner in Parchman, Mississippi, recalls: "Five men have been executed since I've been here, and every time I think it could be me, so it depresses me." The mother of T., incarcerated for 15 years on death row in Livingston, Texas, says: "His illusions are disappearing; with each execution, he dies a little more. He tries not to think about it, he thinks about his family, his children he can't raise."

The death penalty, conceived in this way, is not just the negation of life, it is the negation of beings and their feelings, in favor of a people who clamor for tears and death to satiate their fears and hatreds. Once again, this is the totemic dimension of the death penalty in a democracy. A symbolic expiatory value that gives the illusion of protecting society by eliminating dangerous deviants, a ceremonial killing carried out as part of a spectacle reserved for a few initiates, which the judicial system will give measured publicity to, but necessary to inform citizens about the works of power in a democratic country. Rick Halperin reminds us, "Everyone here supports the death penalty, Democrats, Republicans, whites and blacks, heterosexuals or homosexuals, they've grown up with the idea that we can kill people, that it's something good for us."

After the blood has been spilled, citizens need to be informed so that capital punishment can be given the full dimension of justice accomplished that American society expects of it. With solemnity, following the execution of Ronnie Lee Gardner by shooting on June 16, 2010, Tom Patterson, Director of the Utah Department of Corrections, gave these details at the press conference held at one o'clock in the morning following the execution. "At midnight, Mr. Gardner left the observation cell and was led to the execution chamber. He was escorted by staff from the Department of Corrections. Mr. Gardner was calm and resolute. He sat down without resistance, then was tied up. We asked him if he wanted to express any thoughts or feelings. Mr. Gardner replied that he did not. Following this statement, the execution could begin. Mr Gardner was pronounced dead at 12.17am. I'd like to take this opportunity to thank all the prison staff. It has been an honor and a great responsibility to carry out this mission with absolute dignity and a profound respect for human life, but also for those lives that had already been lost by Mr. Gardner's actions. This act tried to be fair both to those who had lost a loved one before, and to those who lost a loved one tonight."

Social or racial discrimination

When it comes to discrimination in the application of the death penalty, as in the industrialized use of prison confinement, we need to be clear about the elements on which inequities are based. Generally speaking, it is likely to be a question of primary discrimination based on cultural, economic and social capital, partly derived from secondary discrimination based on skin color. This former Texas prison warden admits: "Many blacks were executed for raping a white woman. It didn't go the other way." The facts speak for themselves: African-Americans represent 12% of the overall population in the United States, and 42% of those sentenced to death[40].

Race is a constant parameter in the United States, both in everyday life and in all administrative and statistical processes. Whereas in European countries, it is strictly forbidden to keep records of individuals according to their origin, in the United States the official classification of individuals making up the social melting pot is displayed. It is therefore possible to draw up precise statistics on the functioning of the criminal justice system according to *race*: white, African-American, Latin-American, Asian and Native American.

---

40. *Facts about the Death Penalty*, Death Penalty Information Center, updated August 13, 2010.

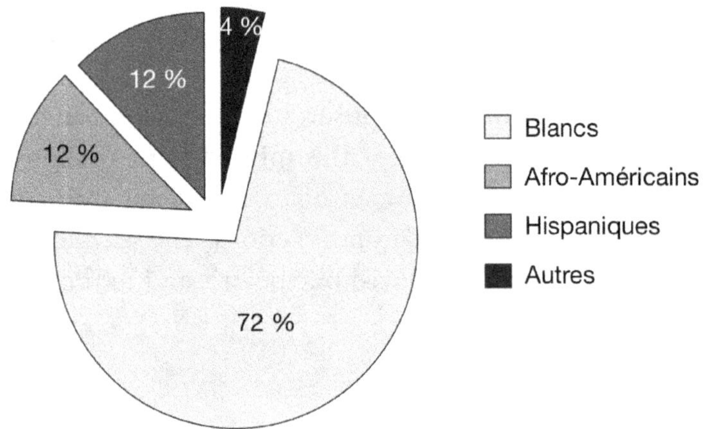

Distribution of ethnic origins in the United States[41]

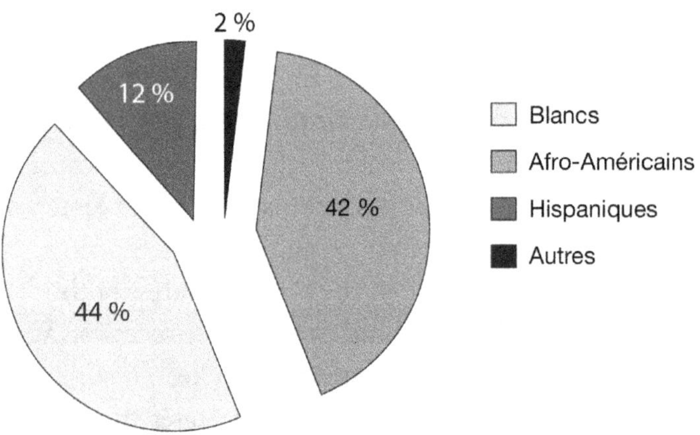

Breakdown of ethnic origins on death row[42]

From this visibility of racial trajectories in the U.S., it becomes obvious that the criminal who kills a white person will be punished more severely than the one who kills a black person. Nationally, the

---

41. US Census bureau, updated November 4, 2010.

42. *Facts about the Death Penalty*, Death Penalty Information Center, updated December 17, 2010.

majority of victims are not white. Yet 80% of death sentences are handed down to murderers of white Americans[43]. This observation shows, on the one hand, that the death penalty is a system that predominantly serves white people[44], and on the other hand, that life does not have the same price depending on the color of one's skin or one's financial capabilities.

Convicts executed for interracial crimes[45]

In the United States, it's clear that a white man's life is worth more than a black man's, like a resurgence of slavery that has never been appeased. This prompts Rick Halperin to sum up the situation as follows: "Equal justice is engraved on the pediment of the Supreme Court, but this concept has never existed in our justice system, because the law has always been used to discriminate against people of color, Catholics, Jews, women. That's the history of America, to benefit the privilege of rich white men. And today it's the same with

---

43. Dow (David R.), *Executed on a Technicality, Lethal Injustice on America's Death Row*, Boston, Beacon Press, 2005, p. 195.

44. *Facts about the Death Penalty*, figures from the Death Penalty Information Center, updated December 17, 2010.

45. Dow (David R.), *op. cit.* p. 195.

lesbians and gays: justice is anything but fair, but people don't know it and they don't care."

Added to this idea, which dangerously mixes economics and justice, are racist claims against the Latin Americans who populate American prisons at the expense of the American taxpayer. Whites would like to see them returned to Mexico or elsewhere, to serve their sentences in their "shitty prisons", meaning in their poor, underdeveloped countries, from which they should never have left. For many WASPs[46], nationality means little when skin color is a reminder of another place. Racism takes hold wherever it can, and assimilation of a growing population from Spanish-speaking countries is not a given. Moreover, activists claim that in terms of living conditions on death row, Latin Americans are often treated even worse than African-Americans. Their condemnation confirms the failure of integration and the supposed nature of immigration: "These men leave their country to come and wreak havoc here," says this young student from Huntsville, Texas. Personal questions about the death penalty very often conjure up immigration issues. It's as if it were impossible to dissociate the criminal sentence, whatever it may be, from society's intrinsic need to identify scapegoats. Evil is not at home, it is in the other, the different, the one from elsewhere, the one with whom the certainty of belonging to the same species is more dubious, more fragile. So it's hardly surprising that poor African-Americans, Latin Americans and native Americans[47] make up the majority of the population locked up on death row.

The racial debate, which began with the civil rights movement and was embodied by figures such as Malcolm X and Martin Luther King, has gained new momentum with the election of Barack Obama. At the helm of power, a president legitimizes the existence of African-Americans with half his blood, in a nation whose bichromy remains

---

46. White Anglo-Saxon Protestant.
47. American Indians.

difficult to come to terms with. Today, their predominantly unfavorable status in society can be better expressed. However, the strong coloring of death row and prisons in general is not ignored by the poorest. This is undoubtedly one of the explanations for the fact that, without having carried out a survey, and all other things being equal, in proportion to white people, the vast majority of African-Americans have a highly critical view of the death penalty. In a 2007 report[48], the Death Penalty Information Center noted that 75% of blacks were in favor of a moratorium on executions[49]. However, their mobilization in favor of abolition is extremely low, as if they were detached from the need to advance a debate that concerns them with relative priority.

History and the whiff of slavery

> "Today, the United States incarcerates a larger percentage of the black population than South Africa did at the height of the apartheid regime. Today, more black citizens are disenfranchised than at the time of the vote on the 15th Amendment, which granted African Americans the right to vote in 1870."[50]

Eighty percent of executions in the USA are carried out in the Southern states, i.e. the former Confederate states, where slavery has

---

48. DIETER (Richard C.), *A Crisis in Confidence, Americans' Doubts about the Death Penalty*, report by the Death Penalty Information Center, based on a national opinion poll, June 2007.

49. In an October 2010 Gallup poll, "the largest proportion of death penalty supporters are men (71%), white (69%), with Republican sympathies (78%). But women are also overwhelmingly in favor (58%), as are non-white respondents (55%) and Democratic supporters (55%). [...] In this poll, the institute recalls the permanence of support for the death penalty in the United States over the past 75 years. When Gallup began studying the death penalty in 1936, 59% of Americans approved of it, compared with 38% who opposed it. After falling below the average (between 47 and 49% in favor) between 1954 and 1972, support for the death penalty rose drastically to 80% in 1994", AFP dispatch, November 9, 2010.

50. ALEXANDER (Michelle), *The New Jim Crow: Mass Incarceration in the Age of Colorblindness*, New York, New Press Edition, Fall 2009.

left its most enduring mark. There's no doubt about the direct link between slavery and capital punishment, as Rick Halperin explains: "Most Americans know that we had slavery, it's part of our past. But most Americans have no geographical knowledge, and they don't make the connection between slavery, racial discrimination and the modern justice system. Yet they are completely linked. It was discrimination based on skin color, and people think that's not America today, but nothing has changed!" The death penalty in the U.S. is also the direct heir to the numerous episodes of public lynching, which constituted spectacles of collective racist outburst until 1968, the high point of the African-American emancipation movement. Between 1882 and 1968, 4,742 black men and women were lynched, half of them in Mississippi, Georgia, Texas, Alabama and Louisiana. Lynching consisted of the summary execution of a person, an accused, without a regular trial and by collective decision, by inflicting severe violence on that person as part of a public spectacle. Lynchings were organized mainly by the Ku Klux Klan, in reaction to President Lincoln's desire to abolish slavery. Often lynchings were motivated by the pretext of punishing a black man accused of raping a white woman. In reality, imaginary acts were enough to motivate these violent instincts. Mobs would even go so far as to drag defendants out of sheriffs' cells, to stage racial violence under the pretext of private justice. The police and all institutions were fully involved in these public practices, during which no one hid. Photographs were taken, and some were even turned into souvenir postcards that the U.S. Postal Service agreed to send until 1908. Occasionally, teachers would allow children to witness these tortures, which could involve mutilation (especially sexual), lacerations, burning at the stake, hanging, etc. Between 1882 and 1927, 92 women were lynched to death. These shows, aimed at white people, were denounced by people of all colors. In 1939, the success of the song *Strange Fruit*, first sung by Billie Holiday[51], expressed the ignominy of these practices.

---

51. Later, Nina Simone would sing this song alongside Martin Luther King, and when he was assassinated, she in turn incited the armed struggle between blacks and whites.

The black community organized itself into two movements. One was a peaceful movement led by Martin Luther King, while the other, led by the Black Panthers, encouraged people to take up arms. Today, these episodes of extreme violence are largely unknown to the general public. However, the Ku Klux Klan still exists illegally in the United States, with numerous active groups, particularly in the Southern states. It's important to bear in mind that many of those who witnessed or took part in these atrocities are still alive. James Willett, former warden of Walls Prison in Huntsville, Texas, gives a half-hearted account of these episodes: "In the 1940s, convicts spent an average of three months on death row. Exceptionally, they would stay for 10 months, in which case the media would mention it. There were appeals, but it was quick. In those days, convicts were hanged. Each county applied hanging as it saw fit, some did public executions, organized by the sheriff, even back when the electric chair existed."

These practices are rarely mentioned by the American public. They bring with them a cohort of guilt that everyone has been striving to forget since the civil rights movement launched between 1945 and 1970 to put an end to segregation. Yet the denial of the right to life, so frequently applied to people of color, notably in defense of offenses against white people, takes the same forms as the denial of humanity to slaves. The map of today's retentionist states shows that it is still difficult to consider abolition where slavery reigned supreme for so many years. As the figures show, the death penalty, as a political instrument, remains a power predominantly used by whites "to dominate, under the guise of punishment, African-Americans, but also Latin Americans", according to David Atwood's conclusions. Moreover, he adds, "You still see 'Legalize Lynching' signs, but not just to start hanging people from trees again; it's a way of controlling, dominating and holding the population in fear."

The distribution of culture and wealth does not allow minorities of color to enjoy the same rights as whites. This is a bitter observation, since it calls into question the integration effort that some would already like to consider complete. It also stems from the fact that the justice system, and in particular the prosecution process, is predominantly in white hands. A study published by the Death Penalty Information Center in 1998[52] counted 1,794 white District Attorneys, compared with 22 African-Americans and 22 Latinos. There is also evidence that blacks are poorly represented on juries, their candidacy actually being rejected without any obligation to state reasons, for fear that they would refuse to vote for a death sentence for a black defendant. The reverse is not true. Lindy, a juror in a death penalty case in Mississippi, recounts how the jury was recruited. She was a pro-death penalty conservative Republican before this trial. She has since become a staunch abolitionist: "When I arrived at the courthouse for jury selection, there must have been 200 people. Maybe 30% were black. In the end, no blacks were kept on the jury. I didn't think much of it, because the convict was white, but then I realized that here in the southern states, blacks are predominantly Democrats and favor life imprisonment over the death penalty. I think as far as I was concerned, I fit the criteria they were looking for, a 'white collar' employee." Very officially, "in 82% of studies, the race of the victim affected the likelihood that the death penalty would be sought or obtained, so those who kill whites are more likely to be sentenced to death than those who kill blacks"[53]. Since 1976, 15 white people have been executed for killing black people, while 244 black people have been executed for killing white people. It's always difficult to incriminate skin color as a primary factor of discrimination, when economic and cultural conditions enable some people to be less delinquent, to disguise their delinquency with greater ease or, above all, to have access to a quality defense. Nevertheless, these figures pit racial groups against each other in an inequitable manner. This observation is not

---

52. Dieter (Richard C.), Esq. Executive Director, Death Penalty Information Center, June 1998.

53. *Death Penalty Sentencing*, United States General Accounting Office, February 1990.

confined to death penalty issues. It covers the entire functioning of justice, and we have to admit the deafness of the American people to explain the lack of criticism of capital punishment from this angle: "When people of color are killed in an inner city, when homeless people are killed, when the 'least of these' are killed, the District Attorneys do not seek to avenge their deaths. Black, Hispanic, or from poor families, when one of their loved ones has been killed, they not only don't expect the District Attorney to seek the death penalty - because of course it's expensive and time-consuming - they're surprised that the case is simply heard."[54] Many retentionists believe, without questioning the use of the death penalty, that this situation is indeed scandalous. Others justify it, without any desire to do anything about it, on the grounds that white people commit less crime. In any case, no one sees in it the sign that such an irreversible sentence underlines the political weight of justice and the uncontrollable slippage of its dysfunction and corruption. The death penalty takes on the parameters of a paroxysmal will to dominate, since it involves the vital process. Without even mentioning executions, the conduct of trials under these conditions, where the prosecution is in the hands of white people, and the procedural errors orchestrated by predominantly white courts after arrest by police officers of the same color, enable the rulers, if need be, to hold a political instrument under the guise of justice, allowing them to muzzle any opposition. Behind the argument of justice rendered, this is a thinly disguised way of perpetuating the domination of some by others. Guilty or innocent, the case of Mumia Abu-Jamal is an illustration of this, a standard carried by the media to represent the hundreds of others dominated in the silence of American penitentiary alcoves. These facts mar the face of a country of freedom in which everyone has a chance. Yet they are irrefutable, disturbing, and flagrantly denounce the extent to which freedom and justice are no more than words whose definition

---

54. PREJEAN (Sister Helen), "Would Jesus pull the switch?", *Salt of the Earth*, March/April 1997.

and operation operate on a variable geometry, in the United States no doubt more than anywhere else.

Abolitionism and the political divide

Generally speaking, Democrats are more in favor of abolition than Republicans. New Jersey, Illinois and New Mexico, for example, have recently abolished the death penalty. Given the weight of conservatives, it's unlikely that Republicans will ever take the abolition project national. This political divide is not, however, a principle on which the abolitionist movement could rely when making an electoral political choice. In fact, American activists draw their strength from both camps, and from the fact that they generally frame the debate from a pragmatic rather than ideological standpoint, without ever allowing themselves to be colored by politics. The scale of the abolitionist struggle is too great to tolerate the omission of certain combatants. However, there have been developments. For example, the current governors of Maryland and Virginia were recently elected after asserting their abolitionist positions during their election campaigns.

Breakdown of opinions on the death penalty by political persuasion[55]

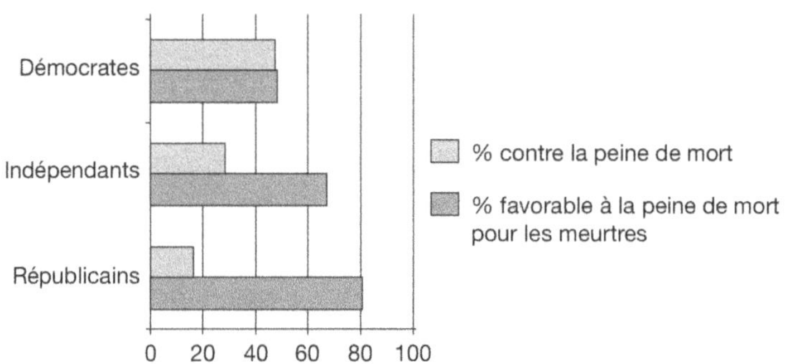

---

55. Gallup Poll, 1-4, 2009.

Death penalty and human rights: a random combination

In the U.S., it's as if human rights, often accused of being a Eurocentric concept, had only a distant value in the minds of citizens. Among the various people we met, the expression is never mentioned on its own, except by Rick Halperin: "Out of 3,000 universities or colleges, there are only 19 programs to study human rights in my country. When we talk about it, it's to evoke a foreign country to which we are opposed: China, Iraq, Iran, North Korea. On the contrary, we should be pointing the finger at ourselves, because we have a real problem with human rights. We're in denial about what we allow ourselves to do to human beings, and that's our difficulty." Retentionists explain that the death penalty is not generally perceived as a contradiction to human rights. For the defenders of this relatively widespread idea, the death penalty is a sentence that has always existed, as an extension of life imprisonment, to punish the most serious crimes as a deterrent. This non-questioning of a phenomenon provided for by law echoes the reasoning of Christians, who see no contradiction between killing in the name of justice on the one hand, and the sixth commandment "thou shalt not kill" on the other. These opinions are based on the same line of reasoning, a line of reasoning that allows us to distinguish between unquestionable, uncriticizable, dogmatic law and parallel ethics. One pre-exists the other, but both are part of an immutable institution. The abolitionist movement must compose its arguments around these asserted illogicalities. The aim is to gradually weaken them, so as not to generate a radical opposition that would relegate abolition to a posture tainted by modernism and all its attendant criticisms, in a country where conservatism has a platform and extensive powers. This is why the strategy chosen by the abolitionist movement since it emerged in the United States some 20 years ago has been to gradually advance the cause by striving to make the application of capital punishment in specific cases indecent. It's an incremental strategy that generates benefits in stages. It took 13 years to convince Americans and politicians that the mentally retarded should not be executed. It took

17 years to convince Americans and politicians that guilty people who were minors at the time of the crime should not be killed. Since a 2005 ruling[56], the U.S. Supreme Court has prohibited the death penalty. Twenty-two of them, however, had already been executed under these circumstances since 1976, for crimes committed when they were still minors.

Each evolution is a moral posture, aimed at deciding that it is not right to apply the death penalty to a particular type of individual. Such developments are undeniably inspired by the philosophical approach to human rights, but there is still nothing that would allow the US Supreme Court to establish a contradiction between respect for the right to life and the effective right to execute.

Today, abolitionists are working on the case of the mentally ill, who represent a large proportion of death row inmates. A significant proportion of psychiatric pathologies lead individuals to commit crimes punishable by death. As in many countries, prisons and death rows are clearly tending to replace mental health care institutions[57]. In all cases, the prison response is preferred, as it is more satisfactory to public opinion and less costly. Mumia Abu-Jamal, incarcerated for 29 years on Pennsylvania's death row, analyzes the situation of the mentally ill in prison as follows: "The problem of mental illness is death row itself, the fact of being locked up with no other horizon than execution, of having to fight an all-powerful system without weapons. Medication can't help; it's mainly the addicts who take it. This is no place for the mentally ill.

---

56. U.S. Supreme Court, "Roper v. Simmons" 543 U.S. 551 (2005).

57. According to the Bureau of Justice Statistics, 56% of state prisoners and 45% of federal prisoners show symptoms or have a recent history of mental problems. "Mental illness, human rights, and US prisons", statement by Human Rights Watch in testimony before the Senate Judiciary Committee's Subcommittee on Human Rights and the Law, September 22, 2009.

The U.S. Supreme Court has prohibited the execution of the mentally ill if experts certify that the death row inmate lacks a "rational/conscious understanding of the sentence and its execution" likely to render him or her "competent" to be executed. In practice, this judgment is left to state interpretation and judicial discretion. Dennis Longmire, Professor of Criminology at the University of Huntsville in Texas, says: "The question is, what constitutes mental illness? It's unconstitutional to execute them, but the Supreme Court has given no real definition." The reality of these hearings, involving judges, prosecutors and psychiatric experts[58], sometimes gives the spectacle of a complete judicial parody, as witnessed on June 28, 2010, during the trial psychiatric evaluation hearing of Jonathan Marcus Green at Conroe[59]. On one side was the prosecution's expert psychiatrist, backed by the prosecutor eager to get the defendant's head. He had met Green three times for two hours. His report was three pages long, which he had not seen fit to provide at the hearing, and in which he concluded, without the support of the usual psychological tests, that Green was probably not as ill as he appeared. On the other side was the defense expert. She had seen the accused on several occasions over a period of more than eight hours. Her 30-page report contained psychological tests, analyses and comparative points of view. She diagnosed schizophrenia and a notable inability to associate the forthcoming execution, of which he was aware, with a criminal sentence relating to a crime he was unable even to recognize. Finally, there was the hearing of Green, the person concerned, whose execution was scheduled for the next 72 hours. Through and through, his speech was blatantly and objectively incoherent. His regular interventions even showed that he understood nothing of what was at stake in the hearing. Green spoke of the voices that haunted him, of the meaning of his coming death, dictated by evil spirits who had been trying to murder him since birth. His thoughts bore witness to an

---

58. As part of this study, the author attended the psychiatric assessment hearing of death row inmate Jonathan Green, three days before his scheduled execution on June 30, 2010.

59. Montgomery County, Texas.

obvious psychotic mental illness. He offered living confirmation of the defense's conclusions, while nothing, absolutely nothing, could suggest that this mentally ill man had the intellectual capacity for any kind of simulation. Fully accepting the paradox between her decision and the relentless evidence of reality presented publicly, the judge nevertheless ruled that the defense had failed to demonstrate "by sufficient evidence" Green's unfitness to be executed.

Apart from its respect for the formalities of American procedure, the substance of this hearing resembled a parody of justice that history has accustomed us to witness in authoritarian regimes, far removed from democratic conception. With complete impunity, this newly-elected judge had clearly decided to put Green to death. It took the impetuosity of his lawyer to obtain, just hours before the execution, a stay of execution from the Texas Criminal Court. This kind of situation, far from representing an exception, is a denial of justice and a lie to public opinion, which, though in favor of executions, persists in having faith in the integrity of judges, prosecutors and District Attorneys. It is an illustration of a two-tier justice system: that of the poor and insignificant in society, prey to an unequal struggle against the authority of a defective and sometimes even corrupt judicial system, as opposed to that of the rich, surrounded by experts and detectives capable of discrediting the adversarial process. David Atwood sums it up when he says: "For the poor, the worst thing is their defense, which is lamentable. That's why they're guaranteed to get into the corridors. Then, it's hard to reverse the charge. What's more, in Harris County, all the judges are pro-death penalty, including the Texas Court of Criminal Appeals[60]. So is the governor, so is the Supreme Court, so it's very hard to hope to get out of there. Criminal justice is a vicious circle from which there is no escape. It's a perfectly unfair form of justice."

---

60. In Texas, the State Supreme Court does not hear criminal cases, so the Texas Court of Criminal Appeals is the state's highest court of cassation.

Chapter 4:
Some Aspects of Crime
in the United States

Crimes punishable by death

In theory, the death penalty is reserved for the most serious crimes[61]. This is also the public's desire for an exemplary punishment for unforgivable and imprescriptible crimes, from which public opinion is entitled to deduce delinquent behaviour that would necessarily be repeated. In the public mind, the death penalty is therefore reserved for individuals who are inherently dangerous. This definition is subjective, open to interpretation and ultimately detached from the reality of the penal systems of the retentionist states, all of which are diverse. In the federal jurisdiction, a litany of offences are punishable by death[62], ranging from murder with multiple qualifications, to espionage, destruction or hijacking of an aircraft resulting in death, derailment of a train, treason and so on. In state jurisdictions, three crime families are considered for capital punishment:

---

61. See appendix for specific criminal law provisions in each state.
62. *Federal Capital Offenses*, Death Penalty Information Center.

– Murder aggravated by circumstances[63], for which the authors of the Model Penal Code[64] declared in 2009 that it was impossible to define objective criteria;

– *Felony murder*[65] is a crime committed *as part of a group* (rape, kidnapping or burglary), during which one person is killed. All accomplices are therefore liable to the death penalty;

– A series of crimes, defined according to the state, ranging from hijacking[66] to serious treason[67], etc.

Contrary to the basic justification of the death penalty by the law of retaliation, in some American states, it is not necessary to have killed in order to be executed. In fact, with the application of the "law of parties", conceived as an extension of the principle of complicity, any individual closely or remotely involved in a crime eligible for capital punishment can be sentenced to death. This law persists in Oklahoma and Texas, as testified by young teenager Gavin Been, founder and president of Kids Against the Death Penalty[68]: "My uncle, Jeff Wood, was convicted

---

63. Aggravating circumstances include kidnapping, burglary, the death of a child under the age of six, the death of a police officer and so on.

64. The Council of the American Law Institute (ALI) recently voted to withdraw a section of its Model Penal Code concerning capital punishment, because "[…] the Institute recognizes that the prerequisites for a properly administered death penalty system do not currently exist and cannot reasonably be expected to be achieved". *Membership Council report to the American Law Institute on the subject of capital punishment*, April 15, 2009.

65. Only two states use this term to apply the death penalty. Texas uses the term "*law of parties*", while Oklahoma uses the term "*felony murder*". All the other states that use the term do not apply it to death sentences.

66. Georgia and Missouri.

67. Arkansas, California, Colorado, Georgia, Louisiana, Mississippi, Missouri, Washington.

68. Kids Against the Death Penalty, KADP, is an association created by three teenage brothers and cousins, concerned from an early age by the death penalty because members of their family and friends are locked up on death row in Texas. These young people work to educate and raise awareness among the general public, particularly the younger generations, of the injustice of the death penalty, as this mandate testifies: "Kids Against the Death Penalty (KADP) is an association whose aim is to put an end to the death penalty throughout the world. Yes, we're just kids, but we're aware that killing is always wrong, even when it's a murder legitimized by the state in the name of justice. To advance the cause of universal abolition, we must unite with all other associations against the death penalty, so as to awaken consciences by pooling our forces. We are the people, and if we all act together, we can make a difference!"

under a law, which very few people know about, called the law of parties in Texas. He was tried for murder and sentenced to death even though he wasn't the shooter, and wasn't even present at the scene of the crime. So he didn't know a murder was about to be committed. The shooter, Daniel Reneau, has already paid the ultimate price in Texas, having been executed by that state in 2002 for this crime. The law of parties allows for the execution of men and women who are factually innocent."

In practice, criminologist Professor Steven F. Shatz, from the University of San Francisco, carried out a scientific study based on an empirical study of the application of the death penalty in California. He observed: "I've noticed that the death penalty is completely arbitrary in California. Of all adults convicted of first-degree murder, 94% are eligible for the death penalty. In reality, less than 6% are actually sentenced to death. So District Attorneys and juries select a proportion of these citizens without any judicial control or logic. Yet the Supreme Court says that the death penalty is only acceptable for the most heinous crimes, that it is inadmissible for ordinary murders, that it should only be applied to the worst of the worst. The figures, meanwhile, show that fairly bad people do or don't get the death penalty, depending…" Furthermore, his research work[69] highlights the fact that the application of the death penalty depends very much on who you kill: "If you kill a woman, you're three times more likely to be sentenced to death than if you kill a man, as if a woman's value is greater than a man's, and it's the same if you kill a white person." All this work attests to the fact that the death penalty is subject to the arbitrariness of situations that escape the notion of justice, residing either in the emotion felt by voting citizens in the face of a particularly odious, high-profile crime, or in political interests most often based on the satisfaction of a dominant, powerful and wealthy class. Prof. Shatz concludes that "the death penalty only serves to protect certain

69. RIVKIND (Nina) and SHATZ (Steven F.), *Cases and Materials on the Death Penalty*, Saint Paul, Minnesota, American Press Book Series, West Academic Publishing, 3rd edition, 2009.

categories of people, and in all [his] research on California, no one has ever been sentenced to death for killing a gang member! Why not? Because nobody cares if they kill each other. Who cares!"

Facts and figures

Since the reintroduction of the death penalty in 1976, the American justice system has killed 1,254[70] people, including 12 women[71], an average of 59 executions per year over the last 10 years. A total of 54 women are awaiting execution, representing 1.6% of the population on death row. In 2010[72], of the 58 countries that maintain capital punishment, the United States ranked fifth in terms of the number of executions, behind China, Iran, North Korea and Yemen.

Since 1976, executions have been carried out using the following methods[73]: 1,080 by lethal injection, 157 by electrocution, 11 by gas chamber, 3 by hanging and 3 by firing squad.

Normally, each state assembles its death row inmates in two separate lanes[74], one for men, the other for women.

The January 1st, 2010 report[75] includes the following statistics:

The number of prisoners on the country's death rows now stands at 3,261, down from 3,279 on July 1st, 2009.

The jurisdictions (10 or more death row inmates) with the highest percentages of death row inmates from racial minorities are :
– Connecticut (70%)
– Texas (69%)
– Louisiana (69%)
– Pennsylvania (69%)

---

70. *Death Penalty Facts*, Death Penalty Information Center, updated June 16, 2011.

71. *Execution Database*, Death Penalty Information Center, updated July 2011.

72. Death Sentences and Executions - 2010, *Amnesty International.*

73. For a comparison with crime rates in abolitionist states, see the chapter on deterrence. *Death Penalty Facts*, Death Penalty Information Center, updated December 17, 2010.

74. In Pennsylvania, for example, death row inmates are spread over several locations.

75. Source: *Death Row USA*, NAACP Legal Defense & Educational Fund, Winter 2010.

70

The jurisdictions with the highest number of death row inmates are:
– California (697)
– Florida (398)
– Texas (337)
– Pennsylvania (222)

Death penalty by state since the reintroduction of capital punishment in 1976

Looking at the 34 retentionist states, the following table[76] shows that executions are mainly concentrated in a few states, with Texas in the lead.

STATES	TOTAL EXECUTIONS	EXECUTIONS in 2010	EXECUTIONS in 2009	MURDER RATE per 100,000
TEXAS	463	17	24	5.6
VIRGINIE	107	3	3	4.7
OKLAHOMA	92	3	3	5.8
MISSOURI	67		1	7.7
FLORIDA	69	1	2	6.4
NORTH CAROLINA	43			6.5
GEORGIA	47	2	3	6.6
SOUTH CAROLINA	42		2	6.8
ALABAMA	47	5	6	7.6
OHIO	40	8	5	4.7
LOUISIANA	28	1		11.9
ARKANSAS	27			5.7
ARIZONA	23	1		6.3
INDIANA	20		1	5.1
DELAWARE	14			6.5
CALIFORNIA	13			5.8
NEVADA	12			6.3
MISSISSIPPI	13	3		8.1

76. States that have executed more than eight people since the reintroduction of capital punishment in 1976. *Facts about the Death Penalty*, Death Penalty Information Center, updated December 17, 2010.

Cultural violence, social violence and crime

Crime is very high in the United States, particularly in the retentionist states of the South, where the population persists in naively expecting the death penalty to act as an illusory deterrent[77]. For Patricia Lykos, District Attorney of Harris County (Houston), Texas, this criminality is due to the fact that "American society is particularly heterogeneous, and therefore incomparable with European peoples". For Rick Halperin, American society has something specific: "As a nation, we love violence, we use it in our language, in sports, in our own laws, we export it all over the world. We say we don't like violence or its consequences on individuals and families, but we have no hesitation in using it."

Map of violent crime by state[78], showing that the states with the highest crime rates are those in the South, where the death penalty continues to be applied.

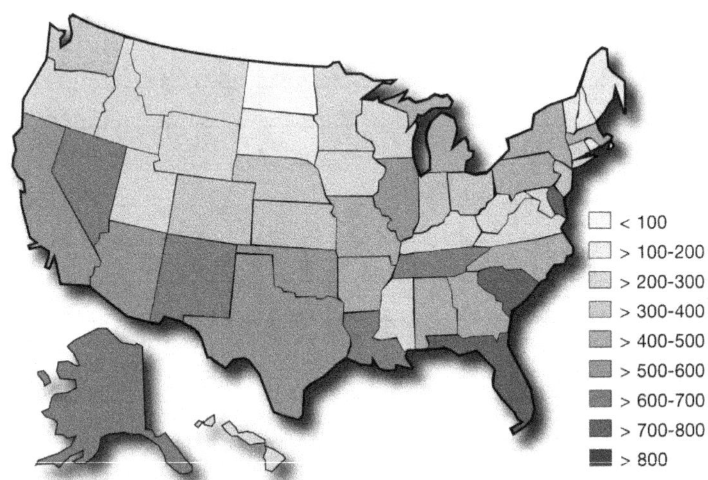

---

77. Violent crime rates in U.S. cities with populations of over 250,000 fluctuate widely. It ranges from 2.09 per 1,000 inhabitants in Virginia Beach, Virginia, to 20.7 per 1,000 inhabitants in St. Louis, Missouri. *Table 08, Data Declaration. Crime in the United States 2008*, Fbi.gov., retrieved 2010-03-16.

78. Map based on 2004 Bureau of Justice Statistics (BJS) figures. Violent crimes include homicide, rape and robbery. See:http://en.wikipedia.org/wiki/File:US_Violent_Crime_2004.svg

Crime in the USA is estimated at 5.4 homicides per 100,000 inhabitants, four times higher than the average for European countries[79]. The questioning of gun ownership, recognized as a constitutional right, remains a rare and immature debate. Very few recognize a causal link between having a weapon at hand and being involved in a murder, even without premeditation. Very few see the roots of capital punishment in the desire of the Constitution's Second Amendment to make justice accessible on an individual level through the fact of being armed. Very few in the United States recognize that violence is at the heart of the human species, in its many guises, that the process of civilization consists in taming these purely animal reactions that belong to us, and that legalized gun ownership encourages the commission of offenses. Very few accept the idea that the temptation to use a weapon, supposedly designed for self-defense, is frequent for those who do not have perfect control over their impulses. There's no denying that the United States is a particularly violent nation. When you cross a street, forcing a pick-up truck to brake, it's impossible not to think that there's a 50/50 chance that the driver is armed, and therefore likely to shoot. Any situation of irritation, any challenge to egos, however involuntary, any feeling of fear and any need for domination can give rise, in a multitude of circumstances, to the use of a weapon that the vast majority of men persist in carrying with them, as if they were in a war situation, or in a never-ending conquest of the Wild West. In the United States, the widespread use of weapons is a means of expressing self-defense, jealousy, homophobia, humiliation and so on. There are states, like Texas, where this violence is everywhere underlying, implicit, latent in everyday life. Where elsewhere, in civilized societies, emotional issues and power struggles are resolved by estrangement or verbal violence, the reflex in the United States is to use a weapon to avenge an honor, protect property or defend oneself. The need of some is legitimized by the presumption of danger of others, under the guise of a particular

---

79. *Crime in the United States 2008*, Department of Justice - FBI (USA), September 2009, June 16 2010.

definition of freedom. Rick Halperin continues: "We are slaves to this fear of violence. The fact that someone could walk into this office as we speak and shoot us all is not freedom, it's perversion, it's insanity." It's a vicious circle that no one dares interrupt, not even the mother of a death row inmate whose early life was marked by violence and gang membership: "I don't see any correlation between the increasing violence here in Texas and the fact that we own guns. We've always owned guns. Me, I don't like it, but most of us like shooting at targets as a game, or hunting, that doesn't make us murderers."

Intellectually and politically, it would make sense to project an evolution in responses to crime, combined with a reconsideration of gun ownership. In practice, it is certain that the abolition debate, if it is to have any chance of success in the near future, must avoid calling into question this constitutional foundation of violence in the United States. It would be fatalistic to think that gun prohibition is a lost battle, but it is an immature debate, especially in a culturally autarkic society that ignores and persists in ignoring criticism or exemplarity from abroad. Robert R. Bryan, a Californian lawyer specializing in death penalty cases, concludes: "I'm sure that if tomorrow we put all these guns in the sea, things would change."

Fantasy deterrence and the cure for recidivism

In line with this relationship with violence - a violence that is sometimes defensive and sometimes offensive, like so many untamed, epidermal reactions emanating from a young society - the United States has a pronounced taste for punishment. Maintaining the death penalty is also part of this tradition, which tends to imagine that killing, whether in the name of justice or in one's own name, is an acceptable and effective solution, and one that we would be wrong to deprive ourselves of. In everyone's mind, the death penalty is the indispensable response to the most serious crimes, the only way to prevent them. The prevailing phobia justifying the retention of capital punishment is based on recidivism. The death penalty therefore consists in putting out of action those who, because they have killed, give reason to believe that they will kill again. In this sense, the phobia of recidivism and the fantasy of deterrence are interdependent. When questioned, everyone wakes up to the surprising discovery that there are countries where people think differently. The question then arises: "But how do you do it? How do you condemn?" This question could also concern the penal solutions implemented in the 16 abolitionist states of the United States, but because this country is vast, the horizons of judgment are limited to the state in which the individuals live, like the affirmation of a belonging or a sovereignism at the state level in opposition or resistance to neighboring states, but also to the more globalizing and less identified federal power.

The death penalty as a solution to social violence stems from a denial of the obvious, which is so irrefutable it's almost tiresome to express: violence is self-generating behavior. Despite the overuse of the death penalty in Texas, this state, which is not the most populous, still has a crime rate far higher than many other states. In fact, in every state where the law allows people to be killed, the crime rate is much higher, in proportions that speak for themselves, as the following figures show[80]:

---

80. David Cooper, Death Penalty Information Center. All data in this calculation is taken from official U.S. government figures published by the Bureau of Justice Statistics (BJS). See also a study published in July 2009, Do *Executions Lower Homicide Rates?* by two renowned criminologists, Michael L. Radelet and Traci L. Lacock. Their work demonstrates an overwhelming consensus among criminologists whose empirical research on deterrence leads to the conclusion that the death penalty has not added any deterrent effect to those already achieved by long prison sentences. At the same time, between 2001 and 2007, 12 academic studies attempted to prove the contrary, going so far as to develop an algorithm to determine that each execution deterred an average of 18 murders. Among these studies validating the usefulness of the death penalty, others attempt to put forward figures of 3, 5 or 14 murders avoided by each killing. These discrepancies in results (ranging from 3 to 18), as well as the rationality of the calculation allowing such projections, lead to major suspicion of such theories. On this subject, see the work of professors at Emory University and Houston University. These figures are also in total contradiction with all the comparative studies carried out in other countries. However, these studies serve to combat the abolitionist movement, arguing that the death penalty *ultimately* saves lives.

Year	1998	1999	2000	2001	2002	2003	2004	2005	2006	2007
Murder rates in states with capital punishment[81]	6.51	5.86	5.70	5.82	5.82	5.91	5.71	5.87	5.9	5.83
Murder rates in abolitionist states	4.61	4.59	4.25	4.25	4.27	4.10	4.02	4.03	4.22	4.10
Percentage difference	41%	28%	35%	37%	36%	44%	42%	46%	40%	42%

One wonders why these figures are not known, when political rhetoric relayed by the media touts severity through death as an effective solution to crime. Debra Saunders, a journalist with the *San Francisco Chronicle*, dismisses the question of deterrence, saying: "There are studies that prove the deterrent effect of the death penalty, and others that say the opposite. I believe in this study, which shows that if the execution takes place two or three years after the crime has been committed, then capital punishment is a very effective deterrent." If this fantasy is maintained in American society, it's also because no one comes forward to deny it. On the contrary, the lie is repeated and satisfies both the institution and elected officials. It's true that it's easier everywhere to prefer the benefits of repression to those of prevention, which is often more costly in the short term. And yet, the research work of the American abolitionist movement is scientifically sound. And many abolitionist associations in the United States know what they are talking about, based on statistical data expressing the dysfunctions of the justice system, discrimination in the application of capital punishment, financial estimates of the cost of sentencing, the percentage of cases cleared, and so on. In this sense, the abolitionist cause is not in disarray. It mobilizes legal skills represented by batteries of lawyers specialized in death penalty cases, sociologists,

---

81. Including Kansas and New York in the years following the restoration of the death penalty, in 1994 and 1995 respectively. New Jersey and New York abolished the death penalty at the end of 2007, and will not be counted as "death penalty states" in 2008.

historians, lobbyists, communicators and activists of all kinds. But the weapons are unequal. Ignorance combined with public indifference is the product of passive censorship. As Sacramento lawyer Norman Hile notes: "People believe in the deterrent effect, even if the opposite has been proven, they continue to believe it. When I take part in conferences on abolition, during which we show quantitative studies, people simply refuse to believe it, even when we talk about the costs." Schematically, the word of the most powerful, even when it is fundamentally erroneous, or the instincts for radical punishment or revenge aroused by the crimes committed and reported daily in the media, will always be more audible than the rigorous work of abolitionist actors whose existence in the public arena is lost in the continual tumult of American society. Despite this pessimistic picture, the abolitionist cause is undeniably making headway, given the decreasing number of states applying the death penalty and the trend in executions carried out.

Number of executions (1,234 from 1976 to end-2010)[82]

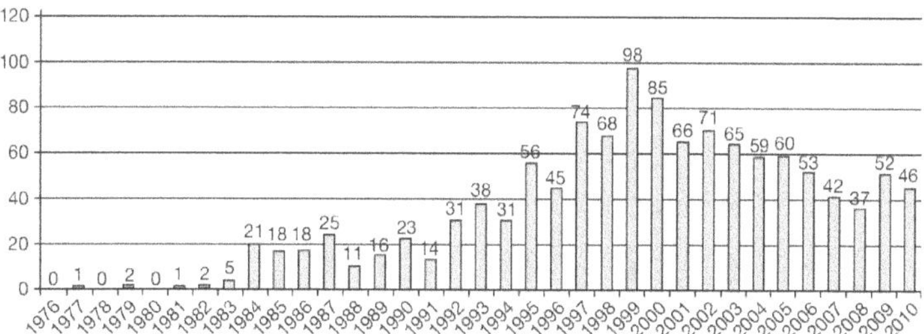

The DNA revolution

To base the search for the innocent or the censure of judicial malfunctions on the mere existence of DNA tests would be to distort the debate. On the one hand, because depending on the circumstances in which they are applied (choice of sample, expiry date of the

---

82. Figures provided by the Death Penalty Information Center, www.deathpenaltyinfo.org.

medium, etc.), the results are not always adequate, and on the other hand, because from a legal point of view, whether in terms of form or substance, the many dysfunctions of the judicial system can take on very different faces: witnesses/evidence withheld, false testimony, corrupt constitution of the jury, confessions under torture, and so on.

Yet this scientific revolution has also turned out to be a judicial revolution. With the help of new technologies derived from genetic discoveries, the whole science of crime has to be rethought. Although the United States is the first to promote scientific and technological developments, which everyone expects to increase economic efficiency and effectiveness, it has to be said that in the field of criminology, the protocols written by the FBI sometimes remain on the bangs of scientific advances. With the advent of DNA testing, this is the first time that an independent scientific incursion has nurtured the necessary autonomy in the rational approach to guilt, and thereby contradicted ancient conceptions of criminal justice, as Steve Hall points out: "Many Texans still see their state as it existed in the 19th century, with strict and supposedly efficient justice, when people had the 'law in their own hands'. But it's a myth, it's mythology, that still exists here. And yet, we need to combine crime and punishment in the 21st century with new techniques such as DNA testing." This pledge of intellectual seriousness cloaked in the trappings of technology and science soon bore fruit. Since its introduction, 272 people in prison have already been exonerated[83], including 17 death row inmates who have been released, in addition to the 122[84] other death row inmates exonerated by other means. This success is due in particular to the *Innocence Project*, which

---

83. An average of five exonerations per year since 2000. *Facts on Post-Conviction DNA Exonerations*, New York, Innocence Project, updated June 2011.

84. These include Curtis McCarty, who was released in 2007 after 22 years on Oklahoma's death row, even though he was not guilty. He was one of the exonerated death row inmates interviewed for this study. Ronald Williamson, released in 1999 after 11 years on death row in the same state, was the subject of a book by John Grisham and a film, *The Innocent Man*.

takes on cases in which guilt appears to be in dispute, and which, thanks to an army of jurists, experts and law students, succeeds in rescuing individuals from the clutches of American justice.

This new means of proof is turning the narrative of crimes upside down, not only those that have been confessed to, but also those whose narratives have been extracted or fabricated by a judicial world eager to find guilty parties. In this case, 25%[85] of the 272 people exonerated by DNA had signed confessions, using mechanisms of coercion that directly indict the workings of the police and the prosecution. This figure, exorbitant in a democracy, should be enough to awaken consciences. In the field of criminology, DNA testing opens up a new scale of knowledge and makes it possible to establish a new chronological causality. The scientific nature of this technique lends credibility to both the prosecution and the defense. It is also a serious communicative tool, understandable and credible to the greatest number of people. With DNA, even inanimate objects become talkative. When a hair testifies to a piece of reality, public opinion joins in. In terms of chronology, DNA enables subsequent reconstitutions to be made, extends time limits in the search for the truth, and allows causality to be explored over a wider time scale. This progress in criminology represents a considerable advance in the mechanism of proof. It has highlighted the fallibility of the judicial system, either through incompetence or corruption. Through the situation of the exonerated, the citizens of the United States realize that neither justice nor the forces of law and order are masters of the truth. The limits of certainty of guilt, hitherto ignored, are revealed. Execution appears, in a scientific way, as a potentially fatal and irreversible error, and the words to demonstrate this become audible. It is on this awareness that the major criticisms of the death penalty are based in the minds of the citizens who defend it or used to defend it. Moreover, when they are proven, these dysfunctions are publicized in the media, as in the case

---

85. Dow (David R.), *op. cit.* p. 97.

of Cameron Todd Willingham[86] in Texas, whose guilt was cast into doubt after his execution thanks to expert reports on the murderous fire of which he was accused. Steve Mills of the *Chicago Tribune*[87] points out that the scientific reports on which the prosecution based its case "are based on nothing more than an accumulation of personal beliefs, which have nothing to do with a scientific investigation of the fire scenes". In this sense, counter-expertise and the gradual generalization of access to DNA testing, far beyond saving the innocent, also reinforce the emerging abolitionist debate. Unfortunately, these tests were not applied across the board, and many death row inmates were denied the use of this new exonerating technique by the courts. In this respect, Hank Skinner, sentenced to death in Texas in March 1995, is a perfect example of the arbitrary application of laws permitting DNA testing. As soon as the State of Texas passed a law allowing access to DNA testing at the appeal stage in 2001, his lawyers filed a motion which was rejected. A second petition was filed in 2005 and rejected again in 2009. On February 24, 2010, Hank Skinner was 35 minutes from execution when the U.S. Supreme Court granted him a stay, and two months later agreed to hear his case. In March 2011, the justices voted six to three in favor of Hank Skinner, granting him the option *of filing* a civil suit in federal court to request DNA testing. However, the decision makes no recommendation as to whether or not he should be granted them, although as of today, 90% of the crime scene evidence has yet to be tested, including the murder weapons, a rape kit, fingernail clippings from one of the victims and a man's jacket found at the scene that does not belong to Hank Skinner.

Paradoxically, even though an individual's life is at stake, the Supreme Court has not enshrined the principle requiring judges to use all avail-

---

86. Because he refused to plead guilty, Cameron Todd Willingham, accused of killing his own children in a fire, was finally executed in Huntsville, Texas, in 2004, even though several scientific counter-examinations showed that the fire was not of criminal origin.

87. MILLS (Steve), "Cameron Todd Willingham case: Expert says fire for which father was executed was not arson", *Chicago Tribune*, August 25, 2009.

able tools to try to uncover the truth in criminal cases. So, contrary to popular belief that this technique would make human justice infallible in all cases, the American rule of law does not systematically offer death row inmates the opportunity to clear their names through DNA testing. Battles with the courts are costly and uncertain. Nothing can ever be taken for granted on the defense side: despite the litany of doubts about guilt, and despite the irreversible stakes of capital punishment, justice sometimes prefers to lead someone to death, rather than authorize the re-examination of an individual situation[88].

Innocence or guilt: a matter of conviction

Very often, when it comes to the death penalty and guilt in general, the central issue boils down to a question of conviction. Some may be convinced of guilt, others of innocence. The truth, if there is one, lies in the conscience of the perpetrators or the accused. Simply, and not elsewhere. This posture demands modesty and humility from those who have the power to judge. Yet guilt is a strong conviction, and the trial by indictment is genuinely built to demonstrate it, so effectively that in a recent case, despite the fact that a convicted man had been cleared by DNA testing, the jurors questioned said they would not go back on their verdict. The disavowal of personal convictions is detrimental to respective self-love, or to the aura of institutions whose reputation is built around presumed infallibility, such as the police or District Attorneys. In these situations of guilt, the facts can sometimes only be viewed through the prism of interpretations that give considerable weight to subjectivity and ultimately support personal convictions. This is the case, for example, of Kevin Cooper, a death row inmate we met for this study in San Quentin, California. Listening to him, his lawyer and his many supporters, there is no doubt about his innocence. His case contains many aspects that make his guilt extremely doubtful. At the

---

88. Cf. "Herrera v. Collins," 506, U.S. 390 (1993). "The U.S. Supreme Court (by a vote of six to three) held that a claim based on the Eighth Amendment, which prohibits cruel and unusual treatment, and prohibits the execution of a person who is allegedly innocent, is not a basis for granting a habeas corpus appeal."

same time, judicial and prison officials we met in San Francisco expressed the opposite conviction, namely that this man is guilty. In the absence of irrefutable evidence or flagrante delicto, the art of the prosecution or defense is to win the jury's conviction in order to obtain or escape the death sentence. As long as the crime committed allows recourse to the death penalty, these numerous cases in which the narration of the facts allows some to be convinced of innocence and others to be certain of guilt do not prevent the courts from resorting to an irreversible sentence.

That's why it's wise in many cases to recognize the register of conviction as a dangerous certainty governing judicial decisions. Criminal cases are often far more complex stories than the media or judicial investigations are content to write. There is such a thing as *knowing* and *pretending to know*. In court, jurors have to decide as if they had access to a form of reality, the one presented before their eyes with varying degrees of skill by the prosecution on the one hand, and the defense on the other. Yet, very often, intangible and material evidence cannot be used to reconstruct with certainty the facts and actions of the accused. In fact, in 70%[89] of cases, the conviction of the 140 exonerated defendants was supported by eyewitness testimony, generally considered to be the ultimate, irrefutable proof.

Judgment lies on the borderline between the narratives expressed on the one hand, excluding anything that hasn't been said or shown, and on the other hand, what each person understands according to their own personality, i.e. their cognitive tools. It is on the basis of the play that is about to be performed, a play in which the prosecution has superior financial resources to support its point of view, that jurors will have to decide on the life or death of an individual. Jordan Smith, a journalist with the *Austin Chronicle* in Texas, explains: "In theory, criminal justice is a great system, but in practice, people are not infallible and make mistakes, whether intentional or unintentional, and with the death

---

89. Dow (David R.), *op. cit.* p. 98.

penalty, if you change your mind, you can't go back." These malfunctions are completely unknown to the general public. What's more, the entire judicial mechanism is ignored, so no one is in a position to assess the stakes involved in a trial, and consequently to take a critical view of the system's potential abuses. "I discovered this mechanism when my son was accused, and that's when I realized that it was completely out of our hands, whereas I used to think that the entire penal system was fair, that the presence of 12 jurors was enough to ensure that judgments were serious", confides this woman whose son has been trying to prove his innocence for 15 years. T., a death row inmate in Parchman, Mississippi, says: "I didn't choose my lawyer, and I didn't know anything about justice, how to defend myself, etc. I felt that everything was a waste of time. I had the feeling that everything had been decided beforehand; I didn't know the evidence against me. To prove that all this was false, you had to know the law, and it was too late after the trial. The District Attorney and the police said I wouldn't be sentenced to death if I said what they told me to say. In fact, they knew nothing about the crime and neither did I. My lawyer tried to plead guilty so I'd only get life imprisonment. Now I've changed lawyers and I'm pleading that I'm not completely innocent, but innocent of what I'm accused of."

This widespread ignorance shows contempt for the numerous writings, books and articles, often highlighted by the abolitionist movement, which regularly awaken American consciences, and which elected officials cannot ignore. In this sense, the work of abolitionist actors is remarkable for its precision and seriousness. Sometimes academic, sometimes journalistic, sometimes militant, this situation is denounced from east to west in the United States. Despite this freedom of speech and criticism, infallibility remains a governing idea, unless awakened by exceptions, such as that of innocence technically recognized when judges agree to reopen cases and reanalyze the causal narrative leading to guilt. But this willingness to seek the truth and avoid convicting the innocent is not very common. Norman Hile, an attorney in Sacramento, tries in vain to save the life of his client,

Kevin Cooper. He confides: "When you talk to the prosecutor, and the entire prosecution, they are convinced of guilt and refuse to reopen the case, even if the defense presents new evidence. [...] The state does everything it can not to reverse a conviction. It's a battle for them."

A matter of youth rather than recidivism

The vast majority of crimes are committed by men before the age of 25 or 30. The figures drop considerably after this age. This statistical reading calls for a number of explanations, combining medically recognized numerical data with qualitative sociological and psychological dimensions. Scientists attribute a direct link between crime/violence and testosterone levels. From a sociological and psychological point of view, it's true that with age, the question of one's place in the group sometimes takes time to be determined, and among the unfortunate adjustments that belong to periods of maturation, according to the education received, according to the integration of norms, of right and wrong, delinquency in general fades with age and experience. This is borne out by the breakdown of crimes committed according to the age of the accused[90]:

Infringements	Ages ·····⟩	15	18	17-24	25-29	30-34	35-39	40-44	45 and over
% Violent crime*	100	4.8	15.4	33.5	14	11	9.8	8.8	11.6
% Property crime**	100	9.7	26.7	34.7	10.1	8.7	8.5	7.7	9.5
TOTAL	7,597, 240	342, 096	1,106, 830	2,597, 696	1,003, 505	792, 906	723, 350	690, 722	981, 707
Breakdown in % of sales	100	4.5	14.6	34.3	13.2	10.4	9.5	9.1	12.9

* Murder, forcible rape, robbery and aggravated assault.

** Burglary, robbery, motor vehicle theft and arson.

---

90. Males Arrests, by Age, 2004 [10,830 agencies; 2004 estimated population 209,671,644], Table 39, FBI.

This situation needs to be balanced, however, by the fact that with practice, it also becomes easier to professionalize one's own delinquency, and consequently to evade arrest. Nevertheless, this factor must be taken into account as one of the answers to the paranoid fear of recidivism and the all-too-common belief that criminals never change, no matter what. So what's the point of eliminating individuals who are no longer dangerous after a relatively long period of incarceration[91]? This is the question that sends pro-death penalty advocates back to their most essential motivation, far removed from a protective pragmatism: above all, it's about revenge, about killing the one who killed, in the image of societies before our time[92]. Debra Saunders, a journalist with the *San Francisco Chronicle*, gives little credence to changes in behavior: "I don't believe in expressions of remorse. It's easy to be nice in prison, but back in normal life, a man can kill again, be nasty, rape, and it's impossible to stop him. [...] What would make me believe in their redemption is the fact that they accept their guilt. He who does not admit his guilt has not changed. Stanley Tookie Williams said he repented for being an odious fellow, but not for killing those people. Abolitionists talked about how wonderful he was, but in fact he never

---

91. This work focuses on criminals whose behavior is considered a form of delinquency, not mental pathology. The question of psychiatric illness, treated in the United States as elsewhere by prison confinement, should in fact be the subject of a different type of punitive, social and medical treatment. In these situations of recognized mental illness, the question of recidivism requires its own psychiatric response, independent of standard penal solutions.

92. Let's not forget that among the religious defenders of the death penalty are conservatives and fundamentalists, often belonging to the Evangelical or Baptist churches, more concerned with preserving ancient beliefs and practices than with advancing society. Modernism is equated with evil, with demonic inspiration in contradiction with a search for contemporaneity with the Bible. Thus, the origin of man is taught from Adam and Eve onwards, in defiance of all scientific discovery. This phenomenon should remind old Europe of its own phases of obscurantism, notably the time when religion enjoined the refutation of the theories of Copernicus and Galileo. The Earth was reputed to be flat with the Sun above it; to admit its spherical aspect and the principle of heliocentrism was a heresy punishable by death in the 17th century.

expressed a shred of regret for his deed. He just wanted to be free in the streets and maybe kill other people."[93]

---

93. This account of Stanley Tookie Williams is Debra Saunders's alone. Barbara Becnel, Stanley's close friend, does not corroborate this version. Barbara is a journalist, writer and film producer. A well-known activist and politician, she was also the first African-American woman to campaign for the Democratic camp in the 2006 California gubernatorial race against Arnold Schwarzenegger. She came third ahead of two other Democratic candidates, Phil Angelides and Steve Westly, whose pro-death penalty views she denounced. She left the Democratic Party to join the Green Party of California in 2007. Barbara was present on the day of her friend's execution by lethal injection: "It was a real butchery, they worked on him for over 45 minutes trying to prick his veins and then kill him, even though the protocol is supposed to last 6 to 8 minutes."

CHAPTER 5:
THE JUDICIAL PROCESS

Since the reintroduction of capital punishment in 1976, the possibility of resorting to a death sentence has required a judicial system that is all the more special. On the one hand, because it is a matter of criminal justice, there are specific procedural rules, investigative requirements and remedies that underline the importance of the case to be judged. On the other hand, because the sentence is irreversible, trials must obey contingencies designed and written by the legislator, with the aim of avoiding committing the irreparable. This difference between life imprisonment and capital punishment justifies the difference in cost between these two sentences[94], as well as the length of trials and appeals at both state and federal levels.

Jury selection

To be included in the selection, you must be able to answer favorably to the question: "Would you be able to decide in favor of capital punishment if such were the proposed verdict?" In this way, a procedure is put in place that assures the judge that the death penalty can be applied if the prosecution so requests. Abolitionists are thus excluded from the judicial mechanism of their own country. In this case, they

---

94. As a reminder, a death penalty trial costs the community four to five times more than a prison sentence, even including the cost of life imprisonment without parole.

are considered likely to cause an obstruction of justice, a justice system predominantly run by retentionists. This is why Dennis Longmire, professor of criminology at the University of Huntsville, Texas, points out that "Catholics and Jews, known for their abolitionist views, are not welcome on juries. They are regularly replaced by white Protestant Baptist or Evangelical citizens, whose morality does not prohibit them from voting in favor of capital punishment".

For a general criminal trial, you need to assemble around 50 people selected from the voters' list or the driver's license list. The judge qualifies them, the lawyers question them for three hours, then proceed to eliminate them by vote, with no motivation to be specified. Cases of discrimination are therefore difficult to identify and rarely challenged for lack of evidence. For a trial in which the death penalty is requested, 200 people are invited to attend, to finally compose a jury of 12. The media, authorized to cover all stages of the trial, can also attend this selection process. On the surface, the system is intended to be very democratic, but prohibitions can be breached at other stages, during the investigation, or by unnatural collusion between the judge and the prosecution, and sometimes even the defense when the latter is appointed ex officio. In some trials, jurors cannot communicate with the outside world, not even with their families. They are all isolated in a hotel with no telephone or television, completely cut off from outside life. They are taken to court by bus, and jurors are not allowed to talk to each other about the case in hand. Lindy Wells, a former juror on Bobby's trial in Mississippi, and previously a pro-death penalty advocate until she was called upon to speak out in a trial that led to the execution of the condemned man, reflects on the way the judiciary works; she feels she was instrumentalized. "I was convinced that I wasn't going to be selected, but I was as juror number 2, which surprised me. We had to give our phone to the deputy sheriff, and we were forbidden to contact anyone during the trial. We weren't allowed to talk outside the jury room. It was pretty stressful at night. Nor were we allowed to read newspapers or watch television. At the hotel or on the transport, we could talk to each other about the weather, but not about the court case. And we all complied! We were isolated from everything that was going on outside. But I didn't know anything about this man's case. I didn't know anything about it. All I knew was that it was murder, and that we'd have to decide on the sentence. We didn't know what it was all about until the prosecutor made his case. It was a very busy day. At the moment of deliberation, the judge gave us instructions, points to follow, to guide us between the death penalty or life imprisonment. In fact, depending on the questions he asked and that we had to answer, there was no other option but the death penalty. We were objectively forced to vote in favor of this sentence. However, I was the only one who was not in favor of condemning him to death, and I said so. Then the others told me that if we didn't vote in favor of the death penalty, Bobby could be paroled in a few years: 'Would you like him to be free in the street again?' They were setting an example of a murderer going out and killing other people. I didn't want the responsibility of maybe bringing about the release of someone who might do harm again later. So I cracked under the pressure, because it was the only thing I could do at the time. […] During the trial, Bobby and I exchanged glances, and I began to want to judge him beyond what the prosecution was saying about him. Something happened in my heart. I began to feel compassion for him. My opinion changed. I felt he had no defense during the trial. Nobody came to help him. His sister came to ask not to take her brother's life, but he really had no defense. Everything we saw was constructed and said to condemn him. And I think that in all death sentences, it's the same thing. The whole trial had been for the prosecution, and I thought that was unfair. But I couldn't answer the judge's questions any other way, and our unanimous answers led to the death sentence.

We didn't even know that the judge was the same as at his first trial! They knew he'd get the death penalty even before the trial. But there's so much information the jury doesn't have access to! I discovered a lot of things after the fact. How can we judge properly if we're not given all the information? For me, this system is broken, it doesn't work.

[...] When I got home, I was angry because I hadn't been told everything. Then I read all the articles about what had happened during his first trial... I contacted his parents. I now understood that there were plenty of extenuating circumstances that could have earned him a life sentence instead of the death penalty. After the trial, I said to myself, 'How am I going to feel the day I hear on the radio that he's going to be executed on such-and-such a day at such-and-such a time?' It doesn't leave you and it changed my outlook. I couldn't talk to my friends about it, because they're all for the death penalty. So I went to see my pastor who showed me the Old Testament, explaining to me by 'an eye for an eye' that the death penalty was something biblical... It didn't convince me.

Thirteen years after the trial, I received a letter from Bobby. I wanted to know how he was. In the letter, he explained that he knew how I felt, that I shouldn't feel guilty. I kept the letter with me for two months, then asked his lawyers for permission to see him. I needed him to forgive me, because I didn't want to be an accomplice in this misfortune... I went to ask him for forgiveness, and he forgave me [...] We all have our responsibility as citizens. When we're called to do our civic duty as jurors, we must obey the laws of our country. But those laws are so flawed, there are so many political implications in trials. So ever since then, I've been angry at the system. Bobby was executed. I've become an abolitionist, even though I'm still a conservative Republican. It doesn't go together, I know, but that case changed my life, I still think about it every day [...]"

The trial

There are two trials, one to determine guilt, the other to decide the sentence. The length of the trials varies enormously, depending on the complexity of the facts and the respective commitment of the prosecution and the defense. It can range from a few days to several months. Then comes the deliberation, with no time limits, and unanimity on both verdicts is required to pass sentence. It is mainly the prosecution that decides what will or will not be presented to the jury. In fact, jurors are generally not inclined to compromise, their judgment is binary and the questions they are asked to answer, written by the judge, are not open to contradiction given the course of the trial. When there is disagreement, the judge precipitates the final decision by announcing that he or she will have to book another night at the hotel, and frequently everyone agrees with the absolute majority. It is also in these circumstances that men are sent to their deaths. Criminal trials usually take place within a year of the arrest. Emotions linked to the crime are still running high. Executions, on the other hand, often take place more than 10 years after conviction, and are often met with indifference, unless the case is particularly high-profile.

So, in many cases, the number of innocent people in prison or the severity of sentences are explained by two factors that combine in a common motivation involving the political stakes of District Attorneys, state judges, prosecutors and governors. This combination of excesses expresses all the potential perversity of the judicial system. Even if not every death penalty case satisfies these extremes, the scheme is unfortunately still very realistic, with a reliability that is sufficiently remarkable to address two essential issues. Firstly, the people want the criminal's blood to be shed to redeem the blood of the victims. Secondly, *councillors* are elected on a platform of ruthless severity, expressed as a response to collective fears in the face of widespread criminality and the many sordid cases reported in the media on a daily basis. The aim is to ensure that victims receive swift and effective justice, as illustrated by the campaign pledges made by Lisa Benge Michalk[95], judge in Montgomery County, Texas: "I believe that people should be held accountable for their crimes. Ronald Reagan once said: 'We must reject the idea that every time a law is flouted, society is guilty rather than the person who flouted it. It's time to restore the American precept by which every person must answer for his or her actions.'

95. In this case, Jonathan Marcus Green's aforementioned judge in the context of the hearing to determine, on the basis of his mental state, his "rational understanding of the facts establishing a causality between his crime and his killing".

Victims deserve better. They deserve an efficient justice system, so they don't have to wait for years. Justice delayed is justice denied."

The embodiment of power and strength, capable of defying life, forcing it into prison or even suppressing it, remains the most accessible token for those seeking election to most offices in the United States. It's all about representing the symbol of a father, a protective force capable of impeding everything in favor of a reassuring order. This is the mission of the institution of justice and the actors who articulate it, aided by all the symbolic aspects of capital punishment, which represents a phallic totem which, as in ancient societies, is expected to allay collective fears and hatreds. In the end, the people demand - and sometimes obtain - blood and symbolic castration to extinguish their phobias and reassure their anxieties, while experiencing on a local scale the supreme domination of an authority capable of killing.

Executioners and men

There's no such thing as an executioner in the United States. Execution is the work of the prison staff, whose mission it is. A professional mission that is an integral part of the position to which one or the other is appointed. To work in a prison where executions are carried out is to be liable to be designated as an executioner, even if neither the word nor the function exists.

The case of the execution of Ronnie Lee Gardner on June 18, 2010, by firing squad, shows in the executors of "dirty deeds", the desire for pragmatism and the motivation of the feeling of accomplishment as a legitimization of the killing. There is no room for notions such as ethics or morality. One shooter clarifies: "For me it was just a job, nothing more than getting an order to do something like kick in a door to deliver a summons," says a member of the firing squad[96]. Two

---

96. KIRBY (Robert), "Executioners share motives, describe their roles in death by firing squad", *Salt Lake Tribune*, June 2010.

hundred men, all members of the police force, volunteered to shoot Gardner. It's a predominantly male function. In the end, five of them fired, including one with a blank bullet[97]. In the execution protocol, the dimension of guilt is not omitted. It's a question of regulating the execution like clockwork, which is also what gives it its institutional dimension, from which derive its authenticity and its distinction from simple, unprepared assassination. The officer in charge of the execution justifies his choice in this way: he indicates that he chooses the members of the platoon for their maturity and sense of responsibility. "They're well-trained and I knew they wouldn't go bragging afterwards. I wanted the best people to do the job properly."

Despite this idea, driven by a sense of ridding society of a dangerous element, the killing of a fellow human being cannot completely detach itself from the emotion that the words to describe it inevitably drain: "My wife was worried about possible reprisals from people if they found out I was one of the shooters," said an officer who had also exchanged views with a clergyman. "I struggled with morality. I'm not a super religious or spiritual person. I go to church every Sunday. I struggled with 'thou shalt not kill'. But still, I felt it was part of my job."

In Salt Lake City, this involved the anonymous shooting of a man at point-blank range in a closed room. While the term *"barbaric"* may sometimes have a subjective ideological connotation, it is universally acceptable to describe this act as violent. The authorities therefore seem to prefer to leave doubt as to who was really responsible for the death. Everyone can fall asleep reassured that the murder was collective, institutionalized and semi-public, but also potentially exonerated thanks to the existence of this blank bullet, one of the benefits of which is to alleviate a feeling of guilt: nobody can be certain of

---

97. JOHNSON (Kirk), "Double murderer executed by firing squad in Utah", *New York Times*, June 18, 2010.

Chapter 5: The Judicial Process

having killed the condemned man. Another advantage of this system is that it prevents some from confidently boasting of having killed the presumed culprit, an intention for which one of the shooters clears his name: "I don't think any of us is driven by a need for revenge"; another member of the trio declared, "We took this very seriously and wanted to do it right."

In other situations, the death penalty forces citizens to become accomplices in a death penalty system, sometimes against their will. A guard at Riverbend prison in Nashville, Tennessee, confided that he had, on several occasions and against his will, been appointed to watch death row inmates in the execution area during the three days preceding the killing[98]. He also stated that he hoped never to be appointed to carry out the execution. But if orders dictate, he may not be able to escape his mission. As in other historical periods, there is this paradox among the executors of "dirty work", who perform tasks sometimes refused in good conscience, but motivated by the exercise of a profession and the difficulty of disobeying the system. For example, Jeanne Woodford, the former warden of San Quentin prison in California, was a convinced abolitionist. However, she had to carry out four executions as part of her duties: "I was always against the death penalty, but I tried to do my job as humanely as possible. It's part of me now, I have to live with it." Ricky Bell, the warden of Nashville's Riverbend prison, refuses to tell anyone how he feels about the executions he's led: "I never talk about it, voluntarily. I don't talk about it. I just do my job." However, his dignified, sad gaze and bent face seem to speak for themselves. The former warden of Huntsville's Walls prison, where executions take place in Texas, was responsible for organizing 89 executions during his three-year tenure: "I loved my job as prison warden, as it should be, I started out as a simple guard here, and ended my career at the top of the hierarchy. Executions were part of my job, part of my duty. Someone would have done the job for

---

98. A period known as "*death watch*".

me anyway. It's all in the past, I can't change that. But, knowing what I know now, I would have preferred to continue my career without having to deal with all that. And looking back, if I had to do it all over again, I'd want to be a prison governor again, but I wouldn't want to do any more killing. Not that I think about it often, but… no, I wouldn't want to do it again." As long as it's just a sentence, coldly pronounced in a court of law, but always nourished by the hope of appeals and the inertia of the process, the death penalty is just a word that sounds almost harmless. On the *other hand,* many of those involved in the execution process have expressed, with modesty and frankness, the extent to which the actual act of putting someone to death appears to be a painful, extremely unpleasant mission, an unprecedented moment of death, with which one must continue to live. There is the abstraction of a sentence pronounced and the concreteness of a sentence carried out. These two stages are distinct, as attested by this lawyer who, for the first time in her career, worked on a criminal case to defend a death row inmate finally executed in Texas in July 2010: "I always had a good relationship during the trial with all the judicial players. But a few days before the execution, I found myself confronted with an enormous machine made up of very nice people who, in reality, were drawing up plans, a whole organization to actually kill someone, in this case my client. It was strange and monstrous! The civilizational process, including in the United States, has reached this stage: the unofficial denunciation of the abnormality of a sentence that is only an illusion when it is a word.

Chapter 6:
The Deadly Imperfections of the Justice System

One of the essential criticisms of the death penalty is to observe the dysfunctions of the justice system, and to accept the fact that beings are fallible. Even if, in theory, the system seems judicious, the fact that corruption exists, that the police sometimes eliminate exculpatory evidence or fabricate incriminating evidence, with the ever-increasing relentlessness to find a guilty party, that justice can be instrumentalized for electoral purposes, are all factors that undermine confidence in the judicial system. Take, for example, the case of Ricky Ray Rector[99], a mentally retarded man whose execution in Arkansas in 1992 was supported by the state's then governor, Bill Clinton, during his presidential campaign. Clinton didn't want to appear too soft on crime against his Republican rival. He also wanted to distance himself from his Democratic predecessor, Michael Dukakis, who had been critical of the death penalty during his 1988 campaign, and who ultimately lost the primary. Given this instrumentalization, Ricky's execution left a bitter memory in the minds of abolitionists.

---

99. Ricky Ray Rector had shot a police officer in 1981 before turning the gun on himself, severely damaging his brain capacity and causing the effect of a lobotomy. A few hours before his execution, he did not realize what was about to happen to him, and was therefore unable to meet the conditions subsequently required by the Supreme Court in 2002 for the mentally retarded: "a rational understanding of the meaning of the execution".

This fallibility is also subject to the cultural context of the United States, to racism, to forms of obscurantism and to the will to violence. Although sadly factual, this observation could have been contested by the general public had it not been expressed by abolitionist activists. However, the facts, more and more frequently recorded thanks to the hard work of a series of actors who see justice differently, are corroborated on a political scale, notably by this decision by the Republican governor of Illinois, taken before he left office. George H. Ryan, in favor of the death penalty for the most serious crimes, but also aware of the many imperfections he had witnessed, thus commuted, on January 10, 2003, the sentences of 167 death row inmates in his state and pardoned three others: "Because the death penalty in Illinois is arbitrary and capricious - and therefore immoral - I will no longer tinker with the killing machine."[100] On March 9, 2011, Pat Quinn, his successor, ratified abolition in his state, justifying his decision as follows: "Since our experience has shown that there is no way to fashion a perfect death penalty, free of the many imperfections that can lead to wrongful convictions or discriminatory treatment, I have concluded that the only course of action is to abolish it."[101]

"They wanted him and not someone else!" exclaims Golda, the mother of a death row inmate who is trying in vain to prove his innocence. "They did everything they could to make a case out of my son, because he had been the terror of Houston. Everything was directed against him during the trial. It was even proven that he wasn't in that gang anymore, but they didn't retain that aspect." The paradox is that the defenders of the death penalty declare themselves in favor of implacable and irreversible severity in the name of justice, an institution which nonetheless makes no effort to legitimize or lend credibility to this sentence through proper investigations. Sometimes, despite

---

100. A few years earlier, under the same circumstances, i.e. shortly before the end of his term of office, the Governor of Arkansas, Winthrop Rockefeller, had carried out the same commutation measure.

101. Schwartz (John) and Fitzsimmons (Emma), "Illinois governor signs bill to abolish death penalty", *New York Times*, May 9, 2011.

suspicions of innocence, the support of the international community and the advent of new evidence likely to bolster the defense, the killing persists as a relentless act. Sandrine Ageorges-Skinner, wife of a death row inmate in Texas, recalls her husband's case: "Everything was there to undermine Hank's guilt; yet, by seven votes to zero, the pardon board refused to commute his sentence or grant a reprieve, openly taking the risk of executing an innocent man." The death sentence is thus very frequently used in situations where guilt itself is questionable, even if innocence is not proven. As Jordan Smith, a journalist with the *Austin Chronicle,* puts it: "In many cases, we don't even know if the person locked up is really guilty. We've probably executed innocent people, now we know."

Morbid recipes for obtaining a death sentence

Judicial malfunctions don't always result in an innocent man being sentenced to death. On the other hand, capital punishment is sometimes applied where extenuating circumstances should allow a prison sentence to suffice. In other cases, arrangements with the law or with judicial personnel allow capital punishment to be reserved for the less fortunate, in defiance of all rationality. As Professor Shatz demonstrated, "the death penalty is completely arbitrary". A young woman who came to see the execution of her mother's young killer expressed her anger: "The fact that Michael was executed tonight does nothing for me in terms of justice. Yes, he was guilty, but there were three of them who committed this triple crime. One was sentenced to prison and has already been released, and the other, a girl, because she was the daughter of the deputy sheriff who was investigating the case and turned in the other two, was released as soon as the investigation began and was never sentenced to anything. Do you think that's fair?" The ineptitudes in the application of capital punishment are numerous. They regularly obey a recurring scenario written in stages, which would be comical if it weren't murderous, and which thwarts this system often described as "perfect on paper", but totally unfair in practice. As Sandrine Ageorges-Skinner puts it: "Unfortunately, the exceptions here are those who have been fairly tried and convicted. That's exceptional!"

- Step 1: settle for a presumed culprit, made ideal according to a certain interpretation of the facts, whose personal trajectory (criminal record, desocialization, shady activities) would make the designation credible, even in the presence of refutable evidence[102]. This was the case, for example, of Curtis McCarty in Oklahoma: "Nineteen years later, the Innocence Project and the FBI realized that the police had committed perjury, but at the time, I was the ideal culprit. I already had a criminal record, as do most death row inmates, which is also what gives the police an excuse to pick a culprit and the prosecutor an excuse to publicly give the 'this man has never been right!' speech." His father, Jo, remembers: "I knew they were all lying, from the police to the prosecutor, but what could you do? When you're caught in that kind of vicious circle, it's very hard to get out. It took over 20 years. It was an ubiquitous situation!" Preferably, it's best to choose someone whose defense is precarious (total ignorance of the judicial process, inability to choose a quality defense). In other words, someone who is poor and uneducated, which is proportionally the case for a high percentage of citizens of African-American or Latin-American origin. Robert R. Bryan, a Californian lawyer, confided that a majority of death sentences are ultimately the result of the incompetence or indifference of public defenders at the first trial[103]. He also pointed out that to spare a life when the prosecution has chosen to seek the death penalty, "you have to be really passionate and committed, especially as the common factor between all our clients is that they are poor and ignorant of the justice system". Lionel Barrett, as Abu-Ali Abdur Rahman's ex-lawyer, admitted a few years after his client's death sentence: "Everything I could have done wrong, I did... Abu-Ali is on

---

102. "One in six death sentences [...] is based on circumstantial evidence without conclusive scientific proof", Dow (David R.), *op. cit.* p. 120.

103. "In fact, with a court-appointed lawyer, death sentences are 44% higher than with a privately chosen and paid lawyer", Dow (David R.), *op. cit.* p. 83.

death row because of me. I failed him." Even if the financial means of the defense are never in line with those available to the prosecution, expert reports can be carried out, witnesses called, investigations into the past can explain events, or even justify them. Yet for many of those condemned to death, the first trial was botched in a matter of days, plunging individuals into a sense of injustice and anger. "I didn't even know what or who I needed to defend myself. I had the impression that everything had been decided for me from the start of the trial. I didn't even know the evidence against me, I discovered a story at the hearing, but too late to work out my defense," says this 24-year-old death row inmate from Parchman Farm in Mississippi. It is also from this patent injustice that some people draw their anger to have their sentences commuted to more lenient prospects. Attempting to correct these manifest errors is the onerous task of the lawyers who take over cases for appeal. They must try to identify procedural loopholes that will enable them to postpone the act of execution or, at best, demand a new trial. Although the principle of habeas corpus provides for the possibility of presenting new evidence or calling new witnesses, in practice these requests are almost systematically refused. Obtaining a new trial is never a foregone conclusion, especially since the 1996 AEDPA law[104], even when circumstances are supposed to require it. Obtaining authorization to carry out DNA tests and to present the results is also a procedural sinecure, in the sole hands of elected judges (state courts) or appointed for life (federal courts), which has already cost the lives of several death row inmates.

---

104. Since a 1996 Clinton administration law (AEDPA, Anti-Terrorism and Effective Death Penalty Act), the possibility of appealing after the death penalty trial is limited to six months or a year, which reduces the chances of raising funds and finding a competent lawyer. As a general rule, death row inmates can only file one habeas corpus petition, and there are strict limits on the time allowed. The immediate result of this provision is that those executed are younger and younger. It is becoming very difficult to adduce new evidence, i.e. to retry the case on its merits. New evidence is now deemed inadmissible. This is the problem facing death row inmates such as Mumia Abu-Jamal (Pennsylvania), Tony Medina (Texas), Troy Davis (Georgia) and Hank Skinner (Texas), who are trying to argue that DNA testing could exonerate them.

- Step 2: obtain the approval in principle of the victims' families, who must be in favor of a sentence in line with the law of retaliation, to satisfy their desire for reparation and revenge. This victim's family from Utah remembers: "At the time of the trial, we were asked if we wanted the death penalty for my husband's killer. I said that the law had to apply, that I would have been disappointed if he hadn't been sentenced to death. But if that had been the case, I would have complied with the jury's decision. [...] A few days before the execution, at the pardon hearing, they asked us that again. My answer was the same. [...] In the end, he didn't get his pardon."

- Step 3: choose a jury, none of whose members will oppose the idea of sentencing to death on moral grounds. Sociologically speaking, the choice of jury is very important to achieve your goals. Several parameters must be satisfied. If the victim is white and the culprit black, the death sentence is more likely to be passed by a white jury, which will find in this function the expression of all its racist feelings, conscious or unconscious, towards a part of the population with a different skin color. Lindy Wells, a juror, bitterly regrets having been made an accomplice to a death sentence. She became friends with the condemned man a few weeks before his execution. She recounts. "I couldn't explain why there were no blacks on the jury. In retrospect, my mind cleared up, and here's my answer: the overwhelming majority of blacks in Mississippi are Democrats, that same overwhelming majority don't believe in the death penalty, and generally favor a life sentence, as do many Democrats. Therefore, had there been a black man on the jury, there would have been a strong likelihood that Bobby would have been sentenced to life rather than death. A decision for clemency that I was then unable to make." Jury composition must also encourage identification mechanisms, enabling jurors to appropriate victims' feelings, so as to better satisfy them. Let's not forget that, in practice, the criminal trial is designed above all to match their expectations.

- Stage 4: This stage is independent of the will to kill. It is more a philosophy of law written to express extreme severity, holding very tightly to form, and authorizing meandering appeals, without ever guaranteeing the examination of facts, evidence and testimony with urgency and objectivity[105]. For example, in the case of a homicide robbery, the principle of *"felony murder"* means that the accomplice in charge of driving the car can be convicted in the same way as his fellow murderers. In Texas, the aforementioned "law of parties", a kind of principle of complicity with far-reaching effects, also enables individuals whose will or behavior is totally dissociated from the crime committed to be sentenced to death. Being even remotely involved in a collective crime is enough to make you co-responsible for the worst acts. This kind of nonsense, which leads to simple, unassuming offenders who have never killed anyone being put on the lethal injection table, is both frequent and little-known by the general public. In this sense, the American retentionist population - those who defend the death penalty only for the most serious crimes, in an exceptional and exemplary way - find themselves abused by a judicial system that far exceeds this approach to severity.

The role assigned to victims

"Victims" are the relatives of the murdered person whose crime justifies the death sentence. Most criminal justice is geared to their satisfaction. Patricia Lykos, the District Attorney of Harris County in Houston, Texas, for example, frequently acknowledges this preoccupation. It's not about justice in the philosophical sense of the word, it's about satisfying the parties who are considered to have been assaulted. As she explains: "We have a special victims' rights office here. Someone from the administration stays in touch with them throughout the procedure. We are now working on 'restitution' programs, but I never forget that the only person who makes victims is the convicted murderer himself." According to this conception of American justice, there is a notorious collusion between criminal procedure and the civil procedure we know from Roman law. In the United States, beyond the punishment of crime to protect society, the criminal procedure

---

105. See the case of Hank Skinner.

has the assumed vocation of satisfying victims, as if the criminal trial incorporated the benefits of a civil remedy. Steve Hall, from the StandDown Texas Project, explains: "In fact, we have a culture that supports and maintains violence, that legitimizes violence in response to victims." Investigation, criminal proceedings and the final sentence are instrumentalized in the service of reparation or compensation. It is a personified sentence, singularized according to the victims and what they represent, instead of being a penal sentence, serving the general interests based on the most objective possible examination of everything that can support guilt in one sense, and innocence in the other. The entire criminal justice system is held hostage by this objective of satisfaction. Jo McCarty recalls the trial in Oklahoma City against her son, who has since been cleared: "Everything was done during the trial to demonize us as the parents of the defendant and to influence the jury. In court, the victim's father frequently made the gesture of hanging himself with his tie, to taunt us, which should have been forbidden. But the judge didn't care, he let it go, the important thing for him was to win my son's conviction, to satisfy the victims, who in fact were never satisfied, since the real culprit was never arrested."

Before a trial, the District Attorney often organizes a meeting between the prosecutor, his team and the families of murder victims. This is when he asks if the family would like the death penalty to be applied to the murderer. Depending on the answer, the prosecutor communicates his position to the District Attorney, who decides whether or not the court will seek the death penalty. Steven Kreytak, reporter for *The Austin American-Statesman*, confirms that "the family's opinion weighs heavily in the District Attorney's decision whether or not to seek the death penalty". He points out that around 70% of victims' families are in favor of a harsh death sentence, while 30% are more in favor of a pardon and/or prison sentence. Symbolically, it is in the name of the victims that the judges will render justice, and not indiscriminately, in the name of society as a whole and the general interest. Other District Attorneys call for the death penalty in every case. For them, it's a matter of personal opinion, and it's also sometimes the basis on which their next election is decided.

It's not so much a matter of making a situation fair by considering multiple factors, including the trajectory of the culprits, that motivates American society. It's a matter of subrogating justice to society's desire for vengeance, according to the law of retaliation, a desire for the definitive elimination of those who no longer deserve to live as soon as their crime leaves an indelible mark similar to the original sin of the Old Testament. There is nothing philosophical or moral about the American concept of criminal justice as it relates to the death penalty. It's not about a painstaking search for the truth on which to judge human beings as to guilt, innocence or consideration of the circumstances underlying the offending behavior. It's much more a question of punishing and avenging the situation of actual or potential victims, all of whom are voters, behind the argument of protecting society.

What's more, while respect for procedural form may appear strict, behind this rigor lies the possibility of concealing evidence, silencing or threatening witnesses. At the same time, the adversarial process appears totally inequitable compared to the defense process, particularly in terms of financial resources. It's all about stigmatizing a culprit, even if the ideal culprit sometimes has nothing to do with the actual culprit. We need to find a response to real social violence. Norman Hile, Kevin Cooper's defense attorney in California, sums up these practices: "They destroyed evidence, they created other evidence, because they wanted a conviction. I think it was because he was black and the victims' family was white." This objective is the only one pursued to establish or restore social peace, without ever taking into account the harm of discrimination, iniquity and scorned morality. American justice often scoffs at the fact that violence is generated in society when institutions fail to live up to their promises. The criminal justice system compensates for the shortcomings and dysfunctions of a police force which, despite advances in criminology and the use of

DNA testing in some states, is struggling to solve two-thirds of crimes nationwide[106]. When a culprit is identified, when his profile satisfies even the superficial credibility of an accusation, society seems satisfied with the work of its institutions. This satisfaction is superficial, but nonetheless sufficient in a time perspective based on short timeframes.

Iniquities that get in the way

More than anywhere else in the U.S., criminal law is a replica of public accusations: the prosecutor is there to convict. In the New World, this idea is taken to its extreme, far beyond the protection of a nation. It's the power to avenge society's ideas, to defend its paranoid fears, to exorcise its collective phobias against criminals who benefit from a dense and varied cultural representation through the media, literature, television and cinema. From certain angles, it's as if justice in the USA, more than anywhere else, is a political exorcism against fears and individuals who are often truly dangerous. In theory, the justice system seems perfect in its design. It provides for an admittedly financially inequitable defense, and gives citizens a voice by entrusting them with the choice of verdict through juries. But we've seen the extent to which the justice system steers the debates, and how the selection of jury members is biased. As this self-described patriot from Oklahoma puts it: "Here, judges work hand-in-hand with prosecutors, recruiting jurors they know will vote for the prosecutor's case." While Lindy Wells, a juror in Mississippi, recalls that at deliberation time, her own reluctance to come out in favor of a death sentence was openly criticized. He was told, "This trial has gone on far too long, the state has spent a lot of money, it's our duty to come to a consensus in favor of the same sentence." More often than not, the arms between the defense and the prosecution are fundamentally unequal.

---

106. According to a study of FBI archives, the rate of solved homicides since 1980 nationwide is 63%, with great disparities between cities. By comparison, the rate of solved homicides was 21% in Detroit and 22% in New Orleans. Every year in America, 6,000 murderers are not apprehended, which means that around 185,000 murders went unsolved between 1980 and 2008. HARGROVE (Thomas), "Unsolved homicide rate rises in US", *Times Record News*, Wichita Falls, Texas, May 24, 2010.

Jordan Smith, a reporter for the *Austin Chronicle*, explains: "On the one hand, the state has unlimited money for the prosecution, it spends insane budgets to prove guilt, and on the other it doesn't give enough money to public defenders, who are paid thousands of dollars less than they would be if they were freelancing for private attorneys. It's obscene. It's very perverse. It's unfair. She adds that this difference in financial means is at the root of economic discrimination in the application of capital punishment and ironically sums up, "Nobody pays to stay on death row." Steve Hall adds: "On a national scale, the issue of resources between prosecution and defense is glaringly obvious. The best example is in the state of Georgia. They didn't get the funding they should have, and now defendants are waiting years for trial because public defenders aren't getting paid. So before they can be tried again…"

Every time an execution is carried out in Huntsville, Texas, there are a few timid protests. In short, fewer than 10 people are frequently present behind the security cordons. At the same time, there are occasional protests in other cities. On certain days, in front of Walls prison, where the executions take place, pro-death penalty demonstrations encourage the American criminal justice system, and contradict the abolitionists present. The prison administration takes good care of this group. If it rains, a tent is set up to shelter them. If they're thirsty, drinks are provided. Incongruously for the foreign viewer, but in a way that is openly displayed, the prison management favors the comfort of the pro-death penalty and remains indifferent to the opponents. There is a clear complicity between those who go to kill in the name of justice and those who come to support this legal murder. This situation attests to the cultural attachment to the death penalty, an attachment supported by the institutions, constituting the conditions for a definitively tainted debate. Citizens are therefore not put on an equal footing depending on whether they oppose or support capital punishment. This situation is accepted with irony and calm on the part of the abolitionist movement, strong in its opinion in all circumstances. It's the perfect illustration of the abolitionist position in the United

States. It remains a marginal movement in terms of numbers, powerful in terms of the variety and competence of the players mobilized, and credible in terms of the rigor of the many arguments and strategies developed. Their legitimacy is gradually commanding respect at the heart of American society. In front of Huntsville prison, a handful of activists are present every week at every execution. "I've demonstrated here with a candle more than 450 times, which also represents more than 450 executions!" says Dennis Longmire, a professor at Huntsville University, who adds ironically: "There's an average of seven people present here, with always 80% from the international community, Denmark, Germany, France… Sometimes they know the condemned man, they're correspondents of some, and they come out of solidarity. So it's a very international street corner. What's more, every now and then I think I'm a tourist guide!

Difficult self-criticism

In this situation, which is hardly conducive to self-criticism, when a procedure has been initiated, when public money has been spent to support someone's guilt, it is difficult to turn back the clock. Even the procedure rarely allows for reconsideration of the facts. The U.S. Supreme Court can uphold a death sentence on formal grounds, without ruling on the need for new facts to exonerate the condemned man. This was the case, for example, of Lionel Herrera, executed in Texas in 1993, whose last words were: "I'm innocent, innocent, innocent… I'm an innocent man, and something very bad is happening tonight." New evidence exonerating him had been brought forward by the defense, but the US Supreme Court[107] ruled that this did not call

---

107. Cf. "Herrera v. Collins", 506 U.S. 390 (1993). Sandra Day O'Connor (first woman justice of the U.S. Supreme Court) reiterated the majority's conclusion that the execution of an innocent person is not unconstitutional if no constitutional element has been presented: "Therefore, the question before us is not whether a state may execute an innocent person. The question is, as the Court notes, whether a convicted person who has been fairly tried, and therefore legally found guilty, has a constitutional right to a further appeal in which he would question his guilt, 10 years after his conviction, without otherwise being able to prove that a constitutional error marred his trial."

into question the validity of the completed trial and did not violate the 8th Amendment of the Constitution. As the proceedings had been completed in accordance with the rules of law, the execution could go ahead. An innocent man was thus put to death.

And yet, many investigations quickly end up with an ideal culprit whose criminal record and even episodic drug use will support the presumption of guilt. After such a portrait, it's hard to admit to being wrong. It can also be costly for a state. In Texas, for example, the Timothy Cole Act[108] now provides $80,000 in compensation for each year of incarceration. Innocent death row inmates try to sue for compensation, often with the help of a team of law students. Few are successful, but considerable sums can be at stake, with the attendant risk of unpopularity. As Michelle Moore, a public defender in Dallas County, Texas, puts it, "It's a big step [...] but no one has thought through how to handle it." Abolitionists can, however, use this economic argument to criticize the justice system and the financial consequences it imposes on society. Norman Hile recounts the case of William Richards: "Recently cleared by evidence for the murder of his wife, the federal judge overturned his conviction, but he's still in prison awaiting a new trial. The prosecutor now says he must be retried at the state level, so he's been waiting in prison for over 20 years. This will be his fourth trial, and he's still waiting. And it's costing a lot of money." Curtis McCarty was exonerated in 2007 after spending 22 years incarcerated, following a settlement between the prosecutor and a forensic scientist. Today, in 2011, his criminal record remains tainted by the miscarriage of justice, which keeps him a criminal in the eyes of bankers and employers, forcing him to keep out the shackles of the inside, despite his release.

---

108. Tim Cole was sentenced to 25 years in prison in 1985 in Texas for a rape he did not commit. He died in prison in December 1999, before his innocence was recognized in 2007 when the culprit confessed to the facts, a confession confirmed by a DNA test. He is the first prisoner in Texas to have his innocence posthumously recognized.

Unequal justice depending on geographical location

Depending on where the offence takes place, the sentence can be very different, ranging from life imprisonment to the death penalty. This inequitable situation is due to the enormous power of the District Attorney. There remains, however, a great disparity in the quality of defense between states, but also between counties. Geographic jurisdiction can change within a few meters, so the same offence can lead to death or a reduced prison sentence. In this case, the sentence depends not on the standardized application of the sentencing scale, but on the will of the prosecution through the voice of the prosecutor or the competent District Attorney. To illustrate this point, the case of Harris, Texas, is eloquent. Since 1976, this county has sent 282 people to death row, compared with 98 in Dallas, Texas, and an average of 5 in the other counties. Even though Harris is the most populous county in Texas, these figures show that the number of death sentences is not the result of chance, but of political will.

This inequality is also little known to the public. And yet, it is a phenomenon of which a proportion of those subject to the law are potential victims. In contrast to centralized states, the functioning of the judiciary, although governed in its main principles by the Constitution as the supreme national standard, is the responsibility of the legislature of each state. As a result, there are major disparities at national level. For example, a 2004 study by the ACLU[109] found that out of 900 executions, 83% were carried out in 10 states[110]. These disparities

---

109. The ACLU (American Civil Liberties Union) is a nationwide civil society organization dedicated to "defending and preserving the individual rights and liberties guaranteed to every person in this country by the Constitution and laws of the United States". By comparison, the ACLU has activities equivalent to those of the Ligue des droits de l'homme, or Amnesty International, while remaining focused on domestic violations in the USA.

110. "In North Carolina, the disparities of the capital punishment system were depicted in a 1988 study which showed that the chances of defendants with the same quality of legal representation being tried for first-degree murder depended largely on which district handled the case. While most districts have only required the death penalty in 5 to 15% of cases, the rate is 42% and 40% in 2 districts, in which a defendant is 2.8 times more likely to have the death penalty required against him than in a county with a lower rate", *Justice éparpillée: disparités géographiques de la peine de mort*, ACLU, March 5, 2004.

also exist at state level[111]. Requesting the death penalty remains the responsibility of the District Attorney or prosecutor, while the use of DNA testing to support a defense is a matter for the judge. Hence the differences in treatment, both in the judicial process governing appeals and in the way death row is organized. Under these conditions of application, it becomes difficult to consider capital punishment as an exceptional supreme punishment, indispensable for the security of the city. It's more like a random verdict, from which it's difficult to expect deterrence and fairness. It is also a situation that contradicts the very idea of justice, theoretically founded on the principle of the *same law for all.*

Table summarizing the number of executions by region since 1976[112]

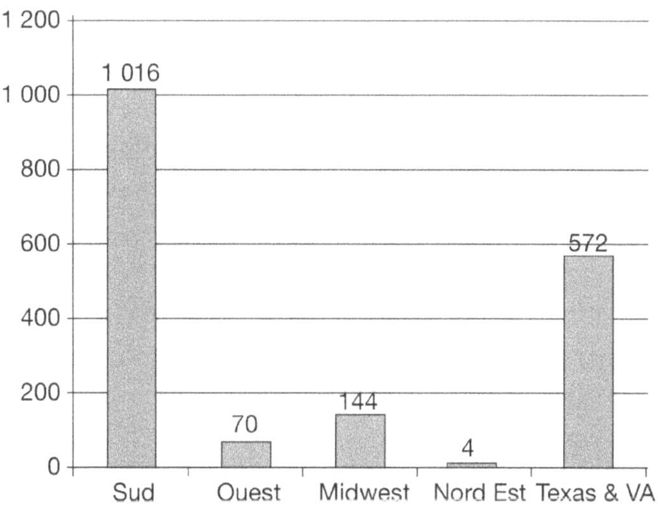

---

111. "For example, prosecutors in Baltimore County were 13 times more likely to seek the death penalty than those in Baltimore City, the state's largest city. Baltimore County is five times more likely to seek the death penalty than Montgomery County, and three times more likely than Anne Arundel County; both have higher murder rates than Baltimore," *Justice Scattered: Geographic Disparities in the Death Penalty*, ACLU, March 5, 2004.

112. Figures updated on December 17, 2010. Federal executions are included in this figure, in the regions where the crimes were committed.

The perverse collusion between justice and politics

Death penalty campaigns are simply the continuation of a culture that exists throughout the United States. We have to be "tough on crime"[113], severe and ruthless against the perpetrators. As the lawyer of an executed death row inmate explains: "The system means that elected officials, even Democrats, want to be *tough on crime* without really thinking about how to create an effective system for victims. They're not trying to reduce crime. It's just a political way of responding to feelings of insecurity, of positioning themselves as solutions to dangers." This reflex has the disadvantage of deafening, dumbing down and blinding any analysis of the circumstances and motivations behind crime. Yet American society is unwilling and unable to question its model, always presented as the best and most innovative. As this university professor from Dallas, Texas, sums up: "We're told right from the start that we live in the best country. And if you criticize America, people will think you're not grateful to live here. They'd rather say: why don't you appreciate it than criticize it?" This credulity is reinforced by politicians. State judges and district attorneys are in fact political figures. They are all elected and base their quality on their implacable will to punish: to find a guilty party and punish him or her without indulgence. For them, it's a matter of representing strength and implacable toughness, the phallic symbol of the father who protects in all circumstances. It is to this paternal image of a political and judicial system that American society associates its blind faith in institutions, often raised to the height of a divinely-inspired system. This other California lawyer sums up the situation after a career spanning more than 30 years: "The death penalty does nothing, except that politically, it's a practical tool, it's a policy of death. When you want to get into a campaign, saying that you're going to be tough and use the death penalty, that you're going to kill people, works very well. It's not a question of what's true or false. It has nothing to do with justice [...] But if it's wrong to kill, when

---

113. A formula that would correspond to the "zero impunity" of the security discourse of France's political leaders.

it's the state that kills, it's wrong too. Yet the state persists in wanting to kill my clients. It's a constant in my profession. In the case of my client Mumia Abu-Jamal, I've never even seen such zeal on the part of the state to allow itself to execute him."

District Attorneys, the first accusing figures in the death penalty process, try to represent the will of public opinion in the place where they are elected. Some use the death penalty by name, others barely mention it. Rick Halperin, a university professor in Dallas, Texas, points out, "Politically, it's suicide to say you're against the death penalty." To be elected, you have to promise exemplary severity, to ensure the strict application of the law, so as to bring the fears, the nurtured paranoia, and the desire for vengeance of the collective to the majority opinions. This situation constitutes a real lock to ensure the perpetuation of retentionist ideas. Lulled by this discourse against a backdrop of relatively high crime rates, the majority of citizens remain staunchly in favor of the death penalty, prompting this District Attorney in Harris County, Texas, to say, "The people say the death penalty is good, so I apply it." She adds, "Paradoxically, the role of the death penalty is to emphasize life, that's the law." And since there is frequent collusion between the police and the judiciary behind the functions of judge, prosecutor and District Attorney, identifying a culprit and punishing him or her severely are two actions from which this trio derives personal political benefit. W. M., a prisoner in Parchman, Mississippi, remembers: "The judge and prosecutor worked hand in hand. I was already in jail, at the top of the suspect list, so I didn't think it could be serious for me, but I was the perfect suspect. At the trial, many of my witnesses were unable to attend and one was even threatened by the police not to come." It's an oft-described situation that's no longer a secret in the U.S., as evidenced by this *Wall Street* Journal article[114]: "Criminal justice researchers say it's difficult to quantify how often

---

114. Efrati (Amir), "Legal system struggles with how to react when police officers lie", *Wall Street Journal*, January 29 2009.

perjury is committed. According to a 1992 survey, Chicago prosecutors, defense attorneys and judges said they believed that, on average, perjury committed by police officers occurs 20% of the time when the defendant argues that incriminating evidence was illegally seized."

Just as there is collusion between the civil and the criminal in the course of proceedings, and in the decisions taken by the prosecution and the judge, collusion between politics and the judiciary directly drives certain verdicts. In the United States, the election of prosecutors and judges is considered a democratic blessing, underpinning the certainty of a justice system that is immune from criticism, making everyone, in theory, a potential actor in popular justice. *On paper*, the people judge the people. Anyone can run for District Attorney, State Judge or Sheriff. In practice, electoral campaigns only benefit well-to-do citizens, as they require a substantial financial investment. Similarly, the power to punish and the public life that goes with it fuel greed and lead to moral compromises detrimental to abolition. To be elected judge or District Attorney is to acquire notorious power in the counties, a lucrative and honorary respectability. The stakes are high enough to suggest effective compromises, sheltered from a small milieu of insiders who move from one position to another as their careers unfold. It's not uncommon to see a defense lawyer become District Attorney and/or prosecutor, then judge. And vice versa. The advantage of this insider's mix is that it provides a comprehensive understanding of judicial mechanisms, as it takes you from defense to prosecution to sitting judge. It is also the breeding ground for the individual interests of a handful of elected representatives, who together remain masters of the prevailing discourse and the application of the law.

Chapter 7:
Prison Arrogance:
The Industrialization of Confinement

The arrogance of the penitentiary power, which must appear infallible in its ability to keep prisoners in impeccable tightness, is embodied in the new establishments known as "maximum security prisons"[115]. These are fortresses of barbed wire dotted with razor blades and electrification, sometimes managed by private companies, some of which are even listed on Wall Street[116]. To want to leave is to accept the idea of being coldly and legally slaughtered, or to cross a succession of metal fences that would tear bodies apart, leave skin in tatters and individuals charred by electric shocks. This watertightness argument is also the basis, for some moderates, of the idea of abolishing a death penalty that would no longer be necessary since the most dangerous criminals' escapes have become suicidal acts. For Jeanne Woodford, former warden of San Quentin prison and death row in California, abolitionist arguments must be informed by this evolution in prison confinement: "In the past, the number of escapees was very high. That's also why the death penalty was seen as the only way to protect

---

115. "High-security prisons. *Supermax*" prisons are the flagship of the American prison system. These are the prisons from which escapes are deemed impossible, or extremely rare.

116. See Christie (Nils), *L'Industrie de la punition, prison et politique pénale en Occident*, Paris, Autrement, 2003.

society in the long term. Now, with the model of high-security prisons being rolled out across the United States, there's no way to escape. So executions are no longer necessary. Prison management derives pride, assurance and authority from this watertightness. In fact, this is one of the raisons d'être of all prison confinement mechanisms.

High-security prisons in the U.S. are reminiscent of vast camps, equipped with a battery of cameras that reproduce, with the aid of technology, a perverted vision of Jeremy Bentham's panopticon[117], in which the principle of solitary confinement is combined with the imperatives of permanent exposure, enabling maximum control of the individuals locked up. Built on vast sites in the countryside, dozens of buildings remind us of the scale of incarceration[118] that around 1% of the adult population is locked up in the United States, the highest incarceration rate in the world. Regardless of a critical view of capital punishment, this figure alone should frighten the national and international community.

Trivialized hyper-enclosure

Although it is a democratic country, boasting freedom as one of the values singling out the country's greatness, the United States has the highest incarceration rate in the world, far ahead of China and dictatorial regimes. The population represents less than 5% of the world's population, but 24% of the world's incarcerated population. With an incarceration rate of 750 per 100,000, or 0.75% of the total population locked up, the United States locks up more than 1% of its adult population. On the other hand, the American justice system

---

117. The panoptic model was invented by Jeremy Bentham in 1787. It is the modernized outcome of a desire for disciplinary confinement, in which the individuals locked up are continually visible to their guards. The aim of the institution is to correct behavior through relentless surveillance, with a discreet eye that forgets itself, in order to achieve a gradual correction of individuals.

118. Out of an adult population of 230 million, 1.6 million are incarcerated in prisons and 723,000 in *local jails*. See LIPTAK (Adam), "1 in 100 U.S. adults behind bars, new study says", *New York Times*, February 28, 2008.

acknowledges that it "oversees" the existence of 7.2 million people[119], or 2.3% of the general population[120]. The prison sector employs more Americans than General Motors, Ford and Wal-Mart, the country's three largest employers, at an annual cost of over $200 billion[121]. If this country didn't have the aura of a "great world power", it's likely that this disproportionate and unprecedented use of prison confinement would be denounced on a geopolitical level. This situation is particularly worrying, since it contradicts the international[122] standards on incarceration, which encourage the use of confinement only as a last resort in penal solutions. Meanwhile, the judicial system is particularly authoritarian, in keeping with the omnipotence it represents. And this authority is particularly effective when it comes to those "human animals" held in awe on death row. Rick Halperin explains: "The death penalty is not perceived as something violent; it simply rids America of its waste, with the aim of purifying America and society." This analysis is in line with the most common opinions: "There's no reason to keep murderers alive. We have to get rid of them." The rhetoric here appeals to that invoked for animals, as if there were danger in leaving certain individuals alive whose criminal behavior alone is enough to define a destiny. Gloria Goodwin-Killian, exonerated after spending more than 17 years incarcerated for a crime

---

119. In 2009, the overall population of the United States was 307 million. At the same time, in the same year, the population held in correctional facilities (jails and prisons) totaled 2.28 million, or 0.74% of the overall population, while 7.2 million citizens were recorded as being under judicial supervision (confinement, probation + parole), or 2.3% of the overall population. Sources: *Correctional Population*, Bureau of Justice Statistics, 2009.

120. In 1997, this represented 5% of adult men and 1% of adult women. These are the latest figures published on *Demographic Trends in Correctional Populations by Gender* by the Bureau of Justice Statistics.

121. This corresponds to a budget multiplied by 4 (in constant dollars) over the last 25 years. *Report by the International Centre for Prison Studies*, London, King's College, 2005.

122. Preamble to Recommendation Rec(2006) 2 of the Committee of Ministers to Member States on the European Prison Rules, adopted by the Council of Ministers on January 11, 2006.

she didn't commit, punishable by death, recalls: "We were nicknamed and considered garbage to be thrown away. And despite this, I was part of the upper class of human waste, because in fact, prison reflects society with an internal social hierarchy."

A relative majority of the people we met during the visits that enabled this analysis, particularly in Texas, had already been incarcerated for a few days or weeks in the[123] prisons, for minor offences. Whatever their profession or social status, most of these were convictions for public drunkenness or cannabis possession. This situation illustrates the hyper-use of confinement in the United States, as a penal environment in which capital punishment embodies the remedy for the worst disobedience. It also demonstrates the submission of a people to an all-powerful police and judicial system. This authority reflects the situation of a society of questionable maturity, in which even citizens, as if insufficiently mature, are liable at any moment to be reprimanded by an ascendant authority, that of the institution and the public force. Because being arrested and then detained for a few days is something commonplace, against any form of dissuasion, mechanisms of hidden disobedience develop, reminiscent of the infantile behavior of teenagers afraid of being reprimanded: "I keep drinking and going out drunk. I'm not going to change my behavior. If they arrest me again, well, I'll go back to the prison for a few days. I'm not going to stop living though, especially since I'm not doing anything dangerous," says this Huntsville student. This situation is regressive, and reflects the degree of maturity of a society that has few possibilities for self-regulation. Punishment can fall on any action, like a sword of Damocles. David Atwood, known for his abolitionist positions inspired in part by his Catholic faith, was also locked up for several days: "It was in 2004, the day Anthony Fuentes was executed. I knew the grandfather well, who had done his utmost to support his grandson. He was a witness to the execution, and we were standing

---

123. "County jails".

by the yellow '*do not cross*' ribbon. Suddenly, this grandfather's wife started shaking. I felt I had to protest more loudly than usual. So I just crossed the yellow ribbon, and was arrested immediately. I then spent five days in Walker prison! I had a choice, I could have paid a fine, but I refused, so I spent five days in jail [laughs] [...]" Against a plethora of minor prohibitions, civic practices are therefore avoidance behaviors to circumvent the flagrante delicto of a whole series of behaviors which, in the majority of countries, carry no sanction. "Nowadays, we try to drink at each other's houses or shave the walls when we leave the bar, but if they want to arrest us, they arrest us and lock us up," says this Huntsville student, fatalistically. Submission to confinement, even if temporary, is an accepted fact because it is commonplace, unlike the exceptional nature of police custody in most democracies.

The power of law enforcement disturbs all travelers arriving on American soil, even those with the most neutral intentions. Potentially, and according to a rationality so elusive as to assert omnipotence, the wearers of state uniforms represent a threat to anyone. Even after his release, even after his exoneration, Curtis McCarty confides in us his nagging fear of ever being associated with a police or judicial case again. He is aware that there is always a desire for revenge on the part of those who arrested and convicted him, and who refuse to admit his innocence, since recognized by the court. He therefore avoids situations that could be used as a pretext by the forces of law and order to bring him down again: "I prefer not to drive in Oklahoma any more, and to limit travel outside my home. If I go to another state, then I drive, but here, they're capable of stuffing drugs in my car, pulling me over and taking me down, just to have the pride of making me look like a delinquent because I've been cleared and they won't admit it. I'm not taking the risk."[124] His father recounts, "One

---

124. According to this Oklahoma-born ex-death row inmate, the state is considered a "retarded northern cousin" to Texas. There are only three things to look out for: the death penalty, oil and soccer.

day, police officers came knocking on the door, investigating a fight on the housing estate. He [Curtis, *NDA*] got scared. He didn't want me to open the door. He was terrified. He knew that at any moment they could try to take him down again." A notable San Francisco lawyer specializing in the defense of death row inmates also confides, "Under no circumstances would I call the police, for fear of getting involved or implicating anyone in an unpredictable, uncontrollable story. Things can always get out of hand with them. I'd rather be on my own than make a situation worse with the police." Far from this assessment, the majority are probably unaware of the continual risk of being arrested. The population is lulled into a daily denial of this industrialization of incarceration, independent of any rational apprehension of the problems of justice. Everyone hides their faces and assumes that they are safe from judicial or police excesses, which are supposed to happen only to others, the very ones who have genuinely done wrong. It's true that prison feeds a lot of people in the U.S., which is why nobody dares criticize it. Law and order is the symbolic keystone of this industry, the economy is its driving force, and in times of financial instability, Americans are afraid of change. "Here in the region, no one is going to criticize the prison. There are more prisoners than inhabitants in the town. Every family has at least one person who works at the prison. So no matter how many times I tell them that it's becoming absurd to lock up so many people, they all tell me to shut up," says this young man I met at a bowling alley in Huntsville, Texas, who feels "totally isolated in his critical stance". There are states full of prisons that owe their entire economic model to the prison industry. Such is the case in Huntsville, nicknamed "Prison City", a small Texas town where executions take place, which alone has seven prisons on its territory[125]. In Waynesburg, home to

---

125. The same is true of Canyon City, Colorado. See the web documentary *Prison Valley* on the industrialization of prisons, by journalists David Dufresne and Philippe Brault, produced by Arte/Upian, 2010.

the majority of Pennsylvania's death row inmates[126], the town's population tripled as soon as the prison was built in 1993. As in so many other places, it's an economy on a local and federal scale, based on confinement, that the United States will have a hard time getting rid of, because it's about capital and significant expected profits, but also a source of taxes and employment, and therefore consumption.

Institutional liners: symbols of pride and prosperity

Prisons are institutions of pride. It's the authority of a guarding system designed to be as infallible as possible. The lobby features portraits of governors, wardens, their deputies and the director of the state's Department of Corrections. In this way, the system is personified, as a power embodied in careers, trajectories, public commitments, declarations and speeches that contribute to the general prescriptive power of the judicial administration. In high-security prisons, wardens are the sovereigns of a fiefdom in which they organize the living conditions of thousands of individuals, often to the benefit of a personal career, but sometimes also to the detriment of the thousands of individuals locked up. The sister of a death row inmate explains: "Since the new warden arrived in Livingston, there have been new bans every week. The daily regime is getting worse on death row, and even for us visitors it's getting harder and harder. Last week, he decreed that convicts could no longer have more than two pounds in their cells. They made them throw everything away. […] Now they've become so paranoid, we search our cars after we leave the visiting rooms. […] I really don't know what we could bring back. They make me open my trunk, as if I were a terrorist. But I've been coming here for years, only seeing my brother behind Plexiglas. We have no choice but to obey, otherwise they take away our visitor's permit. And my brother only has me. I mustn't fail, so I comply…"

---

126. Among them, journalist and writer Mumia Abu-Jamal, sentenced to death for 28 years, who was interviewed for this study.

The promotional film for the Texas Department of Criminal Justice (TDCJ) touts its business through the exponential growth of its prisons, with incarceration figures on the rise[127], as if to express the pride of a prosperous company with a healthy and limitless evolution. Imprisonment is one of Texas' proudest achievements. This growing rate is presented as a success, without ever mentioning the social failure that accompanies the success of imprisonment, or the appalling crime rate for a developed country. The financial stakes are not glossed over; they are described in a confident, self-satisfied voice, reminiscent of 1960s TV commercials. However, this prison inflation comes at a cost[128], and with the crisis hitting certain states hard, the public is beginning to wake up to the folly of large-scale incarceration: "It's us taxpayers who pay for these thousands of men and women locked up. It's really costing the community a lot of money." As is often the case, it's the cost - the main signifier - that awakens consciences, rather than any concrete criticism of the system. Few are in a position to worry about the fact that prison confinement is also the school for delinquency, and that rehabilitation efforts are inadequate, which, in this case, does not concern death row inmates... Meanwhile, Mumia Abu-Jamal[129] recounts that "there are 52,000 people imprisoned in Pennsylvania. It's so overflowing that some are even being sent to Michigan and Virginia. They're going to build four new prisons. Pennsylvania is the only state to always increase its prison budget, which is two billion dollars a year, the same as California's".

---

127. Out of a population of 24 million in Texas, "there are 738,000 adults under judicial supervision (prisons, jails, probation or parole), and the rate of such supervision (number of supervised convicts per 100,000) is 34.87% higher than the national average. The Texas Department of Corrections currently operates 106 prisons. In addition, Texas is made up of 254 counties and 268 prisons, representing an incarceration capacity of 71,962 people. American Civil Liberties Union of Texas, 2010.

128. In Texas, the average prisoner costs $47 a day.

129. Mumia Abu-Jamal is 57 years old. He has been held for 29 years on death row in Pittsburgh, Pennsylvania.

Chapter 8:
Death Row

Death row in the USA is part of this prison landscape. American prisons, particularly those designated as *"maximum security"*, are guarded fortresses both inside and out. The authority that emanates from them shines through in every detail, even to the outside population. The sites are surrounded by barbed-wire fences dotted with razor blades, reflecting the sun's rays like an evil halo around the site. Authority seems limitless, almost free of all legality. There is no room for negotiation, and any behavior is *a priori* suspected of being a declaration of hostility towards the prison. This presumption is driven by an acute paranoia, a collective pathology that seems increasingly prevalent in the United States. Every individual is a potential suspect, and the taught wisdom is to be wary of everything and everyone, as if any animate object were a threat. The mere fact of being peacefully parked on a public road, 200 meters from the entrance to the Polunsky prison parking lot in Livingston, Texas, with a camera tripod on the grass beside the ditch, is enough to arouse the wrath of a guard leaving work. He pulls up in his car, reports this modest installation to the guard post *via* his walkie-talkie, and coolly announces that security is likely to authorize themselves to fire live ammunition to prevent this curiosity, however legal from a public road. The idea of proportionality eludes the prison authorities. There is a will to mark an omnipotence that nothing will stop, as if to discourage *de facto* any desire to know what the administration intends to control. Beyond the concept of contradictory injunctions, this is the development of a power based on a principle of permanent and absolute injunctions.

The image of American prisons matches the gigantism of the nation. From a distance, these establishments resemble oversized camps, with numerous barracks often containing several thousand individuals. Curtis McCarty describes the prisons as follows: "From up here, you can't imagine what goes on. It could look like a factory. That's the danger of losing sight of the violence of the place: it's just dull. Everything is done to make it look sanitized, but it's not. It's also what's shown on TV, a calm site next to a lake, when in fact they can shoot and kill at any moment. And they execute people there. That's the madness of the system." Death rows in prisons are located in a specific place, with specific guarding conditions, in response to the fact that a death row inmate with nothing to lose is supposed to be tempted by more extreme behavior.

Numerous speakers, including academics, journalists and lawyers, explain that their country is ill. Rick Halperin explains: "We're a terminally ill nation, we don't even want to be cured of this disease, this is the tragedy of the United States, we think we're free, but we're dying because of our love of violence." Austin attorney Jessica Mederson adds, "The true nature of this whole system, it's not justice, it's oppression, and in the end it's about killing someone. That's something I can't explain to my daughter. I've told her that there are people who do bad things, who kill, and that's why they're punished in prison. But, in the context of the death penalty, to go and tell her that it's the state that kills, it seems too crazy to make her understand."

The painful consequences of cage confinement

The principle used on death row is generally that of individual cell confinement, i.e. solitary confinement. Cells are very small spaces, usually less than 9 m², in which convicts are locked up for between

23 and 24 hours a day[130]. A. R.[131] confides: "I'm confined to my cell for 23 hours out of 24. I only spend an hour in the exercise yard. There's nothing to do in this cage except wait for the lethal injection needles. You can't even smoke. All pleasures are forbidden. My cell is my only world. I do Christmas in my cell, alone, and try to keep up with life outside…"

In some states, and depending on the scale of trust to which they are entitled or the activities entrusted to them, convicts can be released for several hours a day. Time passes wearily. This is the case, for example, in Tennessee, on death row at Riverbend prison in Nashville, where Abu-Ali Abdur Rahman[132] recounts: "I don't wear handcuffs because I'm in level A, which means that my behavior has been judged correct after three years' probation. So I can wander around my unit, doing housework between eight in the morning and seven at night. I only spend 14 hours in my cage. Levels B and C spend between 22 and 23 hours locked up."

In other states, death row inmates face 40°C or more on a daily basis, with no air conditioning whatsoever. E. M.[133], an inmate on death row in Mississippi, explains: "There's no air conditioning here. The heat is suffocating and sometimes it's impossible to sleep." W. M., an inmate in the same unit, adds: "It's 90° outside and 100° inside[134], it's just horrible and extremely humid. They have air conditioning in their

---

130. This is particularly the case in Oklahoma, Mississippi and Texas: on weekdays, each prisoner has one hour a day outside the cell to go for a walk in a small courtyard, which is nothing more than a cage with a wire ceiling.

131. A. R. is 63 years old and has been incarcerated on Jackson's death row in Mississippi for 12 years.

132. Abu-Ali Abdur Rahman is 60 years old. After an extremely difficult childhood of violence and sexual abuse, he has spent 39 years of his life behind walls, including 24 on Tennessee's death row.

133. E. M. is 37 years old and has been incarcerated on death row in Jackson, Mississippi, for 11 years.

134. In degrees Fahrenheit, i.e. around 40 °Celsius, in a particularly humid climate, day and night.

offices, they do something for the civil servants, but nothing for us. It's a denial of our humanity." Conversely, in winter, it's too cold. It takes unrivalled strength of character to survive for years with no prospect other than death in such conditions. Indeed, the death row inmates interviewed for this study demonstrated a philosophical retreat to combat the pessimism imposed by their situation: "I meditate on positive things, I try to think about the future," says E. M. "Me, I just try to keep my mind in shape, to make things better. I don't need much to be happy," says W. M. There's no doubt that death row in the U.S. is full of amazing psyches that society is wrong to deprive itself of. As Curtis McCarty once quipped, "Who knows what kind of personality lies behind those they execute, perhaps a genius capable of making a great contribution to our country!"

The corridors of death have all the characteristics of a "kennel", from which the occupants are occasionally taken out for an hour or two, for a walk in another cage called a "yard"[135], alone, in pairs or more, depending on the state and degree of severity. Regardless of the collective discussions that take place as words are shouted in the common corridors through the cell gates, this is THE moment for sociability, the moment to meet a fellow human being. However, everyone must bear in mind that friendships are systematically prevented by the management of death row; and then, "what's the point of being a friend to someone who's going to be killed?" asks W. M., who adds: "It's hard to trust." Always under the guise of security arguments, connivances are discouraged by the distance, the move to another cell, or even worse, to another unit. Deprived of femininity for so many years, convicts "smell letters from women"[136] and, like bloodhounds with a sharp nose, rediscover the scent of desire, the kind that is absent from death row. The sexual dimension is of course denied. In some states, masturbation is even punished. Symptomatically, when

---

135. The word *cage is* the one spontaneously used by death row inmates when describing their living conditions.
136. Curtis McCarty.

asked about desire, death row inmates invariably reply: "nothing comes to me", "I don't know", "I have no idea". American morality, bolstered by prevailing conservatism, even condemns the presence of any form of erotic support inside prisons[137]. Curtis McCarty explains: "Pornography is forbidden in all its forms, as it is considered likely to disrupt the functioning of incarceration by promoting homosexuality! We're condemned to a sexual death. So there are no *girly magazines*[138]. In the U.S., for conservatives, sex is always bad." The control of desires and pleasures is part of this desire for domination in a total institution, of this vision of human beings reduced to a physical mechanics of organs[139], denying desire and the social bond. The very idea of deprivation embodies a punitive relentlessness that permeates the smallest details: sensory, material and cultural deprivation. Everything is done to create the conditions for a nightmare, minute by minute. Curtis McCarty sums up the situation on death row as follows: "The principle is 'get in the cage, behave yourself, and wait for your meal, we don't want to hear from you'. The motivations are sometimes security-related, sometimes strictly sadistic; the difference between these two arguments is certainly thin. It's all about breaking rhythms and habits, dissolving the reference points of reified and degraded individuals. Sandrine Ageorges-Skinner married Hank Skinner, an inmate on death row in Livingston, Texas. Contrary to the way weddings are conducted in prisons throughout the Western world, the prison authorities never allowed them to be in the same room for the celebration of the union. For as long as they've known each other, these two lovers have never touched, meeting only through thick, armored glass. Although marriage is not forbidden by law, the

---

137. In some prisons, however, corruption on the part of the guards means that, for the few convicts who have money, anything can be smuggled into the individual cells on death row. Drugs, pornography and even sex can all be bought.

138. In all states, pornographic magazines are banned, while in some, erotic magazines (*girly magazines*) that don't reveal genitalia are allowed, with the aim of reducing prison rape and moralizing inmates.

139. GAILLARD (Arnaud), *Sexualité et prison, désert affectif et désirs sous contrainte*, Paris, Max Milo, 2009.

Texas prison administration refuses the slightest leniency that anyone would expect at such a personal moment. Tenderness is prevented, denied, for both the condemned man and his spouse. No kiss, no caress, the skins ignore each other, for punishment or security. This intransigence constitutes a regulated structural torture, against which the individual consciences of the guards charged with enforcing the orders struggle. Rigid as they may be, the internal regulations also leave room for corruption. The same Curtis McCarty remembers the "little arrangements with the law" when he was at McAlester prison in Oklahoma: "Everything can be bought in prison. Even guns, CDs, food, women, drugs. The guards were paid to bring it all in. The women who offered themselves were members of the staff, and had to be paid by one means or another. At the beginning, there were also conjugal visits, but only for married people and for religious reasons, just because according to the law, when you're married, you have to be able to have sexual relations, it's part of the prerogatives of marriage. But that's no longer possible."

Through wilful ignorance, the American public finds itself unwillingly complicit in the inhuman conditions of incarceration on death row. These conditions apply to both men and women[140]. Undoubtedly, a majority of citizens would have no problem with this regime of constraint. Nevertheless, an outsider can only be shocked to find such a denial of human dignity in 2011, in a supposedly democratic and developed country. L., a criminology student at the University of San

---

140. All too often forgotten, women account for 1.58% of death row inmates in the United States. Twelve of them have been executed since the reintroduction of the death penalty in 1976. As in all countries, their offenses are frequently caused by delinquent behavior dictated by their relationship with men, they are most often arrested by men, tried by men, and held in respect in penitentiary centers whose living conditions are designed and adapted to guarding men. Gloria Goodwin-Killian, exonerated in California in 2002 after spending over 17 years in prison for being falsely accused in a man's place, founded an association to help the growing number of women in prison and on death row. She also hosts a weekly radio program to raise awareness of the issue. Action Committee for Women in Prison (ACWIP).

Francisco, recalls: "I visited the San Quentin penitentiary, and they're locked up like animals. It's an incredible feeling to see them stored in cages like that, and next door, to see a gas chamber with two chairs inside, to kill two people at a time. I had no idea how criminals are treated in my country."

The uncompromising way in which the U.S. has illegally kept individuals at Guantanamo Bay, and the frequent abuse of torture by U.S. forces in Iraq, are also rooted in the ease with which this country's institutions flout all norms in order to assert power and might. Rick Halperin describes the phenomenon of torture that exists on death row in his own country, with total indifference on the part of American society: "This has nothing to do with equality and justice. Most people don't know what death row is like, what it's like to live with that sentence. Convicts complain of physical abuse, sexual abuse, pricks, invasive body cavity searches, especially for women in prison. Who hears their screams? This country is a signatory to the United Nations minimum standards for treatment and punishment: the right not to be tortured, abused or starved, the right to health care and heating. These are basic human rights, and we flout them every day, but nobody cares. This is torture! It's not *a form of* torture, it's torture! This country is one of the world's leading torturers. It doesn't just happen at Abu Ghraib, we torture every day in this country, inside and outside death row and we get away with it!"

This observation makes us more aware of the fundamental paradox between Americans' vision of their own country and penal reality, between the slogans extolling the freedom of the United States, chanted on July 4th by a crowd completely unaware of the judicial, political and prison systems, flying American flags in make-up and clothing colors, and the reality of a harsh, inequitable and opaque justice system. With thousands of death row inmates surviving in the conditions we now know, with the highest incarceration rate in the world, prompting analysts[141] to speak of an "American gulag", and given the unfairness of many criminal proceedings, it becomes sadly obvious that the United States represents only a pale and distorted shadow of the image that its people and its leaders force themselves to project. Jo McCarty, father of Curtis McCarty, recounts, "I realized that my country was not the country I thought it was." His son adds: "My parents believed in the American Dream[142]. They got rich, they were able to live in this nice subdivision where, in fact, nobody talks to each other. But in the end, the system turned against them. They were victims of the corruption of the system."

Different sadisms in different countries

You'd have to be acting in bad faith not to recognize that in this constructed hell, unevenly distributed from state to state, guards and even directors strive to respect the humanity of the men and women locked up to die. For example, while the incarceration regimes on death row in Oklahoma, Texas and Mississippi seem particularly eager to destroy the individuals kept there, this characteristic is softened in other states. For example, Ricky Bell, Director of Nashville's Death Row[143], has opted for a pragmatic and pacifying approach to the management of inmates, devoid of vengeful zeal and taking into account the needs of all concerned, whether guards or inmates. He explains: "I'm not aware that I'm particularly harsh, but there's no point in being particularly severe if there's no need to be. It's also

----

141. See *American Gulag*, by General Barry McCaffrey, dealing with the Clinton administration's anti-drug programs. See also Laurent Laniel in *Alternatives internationales*, No. 6, January-February 2003; *L'Archipel du goulag américain* by Denis Langevin; Dow (Mark), *American Gulag: Inside U.S. Immigration Prisons*, Berkeley, Los Angeles, University of California Press, 2001; "American gulag", *Washington Post*, May 26, 2005.

142. "American Dream".

143. The visiting room regimes at Riverbend prison in Nashville, Tennessee, San Quentin prison in San Francisco, and Raiford prison in Florida, are more permissive. These establishments are nicknamed "nurseries", due to the possibility of contact visits (open parlor allowing you to sit face-to-face with the death row inmate, with no separation device), resulting in the birth of numerous "baby parlorists". The most famous of these was Rose Bundy, daughter of Ted Bundy, one of America's most notorious serial killers.

by respecting everyone that daily life goes more smoothly. In fact, I try to cooperate as much as possible with families and lawyers. My job is simply to keep these people locked up. I have no reason to do anything more."

On the other hand, conditions at Polunsky Prison in Livingston, Texas, have been drastically tightened since the appointment of new warden Tim Simmons. The mother of a death row inmate explains that, despite the fact that she is legally entitled to visit her son, new restrictions are regularly added. "Sometimes visits are arbitrarily cancelled at the last minute. Women now have to remove their bras if they contain whales, and endure a whole arsenal of humiliations as if they wanted to discourage us from coming. For a while, even flip-flops were banned! Why were they? We don't know!" Dress is scrutinized according to the criteria of a conservative gaze: nothing must show desire or sensuality. Each time, visitors, some of whom have come from afar, fear that they will be refused access to the visiting room at the last minute, at the last stage of the security checks that under-line, second after second, the prison institution's need for supreme domination, just as much as the fear that governs it. She adds: "Now they even search my car when I leave, as if I'm going to hide my son, whom I haven't even been able to touch, in my trunk or under the car. I think they've gone mad, but I have no choice but to submit." Whereas in California or Tennessee, death row inmates are allowed several hours out of their cells, in a screened yard of a few square meters, with four or five of their fellow inmates, when their behavior is judged to be correct, in Livingston, Texas or Jackson, Mississippi, death row inmates remain locked up 23 hours a day on weekdays and 24 hours a day on weekends. Curtis McCarty explains: "We're locked up 23 hours a day for 5 days and 24 hours a day for the other 2 days, because of staffing problems at weekends. It's too expensive for them to pay guards on weekends to watch us outside the cells, to handcuff us, and so on. So they leave us in our cages."

No national standards appear to regulate conditions of confinement. There are, however, standards set by the American Correctional Association, a private organization with a centuries-old monopoly, whose certifications are financially rewarded at the prison level. Each state sets its own standards, no doubt inspired by the authority and political vision of its governors, most of whom are elected on the basis of extreme security programs, especially in retentionist states. In Texas, for example, the Administrative Code[144] states: "Each prisoner shall have the right to one hour of supervised physical exercise or walking at least three days per week." At the discretion of the warden[145], living conditions can be improved within these rules, but also within budgetary limits. Riddled by a hatred of the system, but also anxious to give meaning to these days that are all alike, these endless hours spent in the solitude of prison cells, death row inmates practice cage sports, try their hand at writing or artistic creations, when the rules allow them to do so. T. P.[146] explains: "Every day, you lose something of yourself, your spirit, your family. We try to keep hope alive, but it's hard. People compare this place to hell. A man is supposed to grow, but when you have nothing to do, it's absolute emptiness." The management, for its part, is keen to destroy anything that expresses life, any form of resistance against a system designed to kill people. As a result, everything is forbidden, and supervisors are allowed to destroy artistic expression, thus negating the investment of working hours. Golda remembers a figurative painting made by her son, using paint and paper paste: "He worked on it for weeks. The painting depicted a lethal injection table, held like a puppet by a hand sticking out of a sleeve representing the American flag. The management gave the order to destroy this work on the pretext that the papier-mâché hand could

---

144. *Texas Administrative Code*, title XXXVII, part IX, chapter CCLXXXV, rule 285-1.

145. *The* minimum standards for local correctional facilities *contained in the* Rules of the Tennessee Corrections Institute Correctional Facilities Inspection *do not specify the duration or frequency of recreation.*

146. T. P. has been incarcerated on death row in Parchman, Mississippi, for six years. He is 25 years old and not the youngest death row inmate in the state.

be seen as an attempt to escape… There's nothing to understand, it's just irrational and mean!" It's all about humiliating and reducing individuals to dominated *sub-humans.* This is the kind of psychic abuse found in all forms of concentration camps. This desire for domination is an integral part of the torture process, which governs capital punishment, both in the experience of imprisonment and in the desire for vengeance subrogated by society outside. It's a will to maximum oppression, relieved of guilt by the profound feeling that murderers no longer belong to the human species, and that we can therefore allow ourselves to treat them worse than domesticated animals. Why invest in them, if they are destined to die? The prison administration's only concern is to keep death rows watertight, and to allow the justice system to carry out the sentence, or even to play an active part in it by illegally interfering in the appeals of those condemned to death. This relentlessness is embodied in the social functions authorized to express the need to coerce, degrade and then kill, up close in prisons, or from afar in courtrooms.

Normally, the slightest movement is followed by handcuffing, sometimes even leg shackles, and body searches, in which the guards scrutinize the slightest body cavity, with no regard for dignity. T. P. explains: "Our hands are tied every time we leave our cage. We're abused, insulted everywhere, 'slut', 'cocksucker'. To maintain order, they use tear gas; if we don't open the windows, we can't breathe." These precautions are taken, like the rest of a cohort of security measures, to ward off any eventuality in gigantic penal establishments[147], containing several thousand people. Prisons base their authority solely on their ability to be watertight. The power of an institution decried and despised for the humiliations it inflicts must be expressed at all times and in all circumstances. The 1,300 riots identified in the 20th century in American

---

147. Among the centers visited for this study were the following official prisons: San Quentin: 5,000 inmates; McAlester, Oklahoma: 1,200 inmates; Riverbend Maximum Security Institution, Nashville, Tennessee: 714 places; Parchman, Mississippi: 4,500 inmates; Polunsky Unit, Livingston, Texas: 2,900 inmates.

prisons[148] prompted state administrations to define extremely authoritarian specifications, governing both the architectural structure of
prisons and internal regulations. Imprisonment is thus conceived as a
war against those who are to be hindered, even beyond the deprivation
of liberty. Pragmatism and the goal of managing a stock of human
beings supersede human rights with disconcerting ease when it comes
to confinement and punishment. And as terror reigns in the judicial
system, public defenders are sometimes even reluctant to denounce
these conditions, for fear of no longer being recruited by the state
in future cases to defend, or of encountering obstacles in exchanging
views with their clients.

Everywhere, cell comfort is rudimentary, imposing almost complete
asceticism on death row inmates, a regime not unlike the use of
dungeons. In Arizona State Prison, the cells don't even have windows,
so death row inmates are also condemned to live 24 hours a day
in artificial light. In Polunsky's death row in Texas, the only visual
opening to the outside world is a meagre, centimetre-high window on
the top of a wall, forcing the inmates to stand on their beds to catch
a glimpse of the forbidden outside world. Some are lucky enough to
be able to contemplate a meagre portion of the natural horizon, while
others have to make do with a perspective reduced to the concrete of a
wall belonging to another confinement unit. In McAlester's death row
in Oklahoma, the view could be pretty and soothing if it weren't practically buried. There, as in many other states, is a desire to eliminate
any horizon for men and women whose future the law wants to do
away with. "After 15 years without seeing the sun, my skin was dying,"
confides Curtis McCarty. The others will only see a few patches of sky,
sometimes through narrow translucent openings. Those condemned to
death express an olfactory lack, the smells are uniform in this universe
of concrete and metal: "There's no smell here, it's death. It's always the

---

148. See JAMES (Randy), "A Brief history of prison riots", *Time Magazine*, August 11,
2009.

same. It doesn't smell of anything, you don't discover anything new."[149] "What I miss most here is the smell of babies. I'm a father and I haven't seen my last child grow up," adds Mumia Abu-Jamal, incarcerated in Pittsburgh. The green of nature is also something to be forgotten. At execution time, when prisoners leave the death row they've walked for years or decades, the touch of that patch of lawn, that neatly cut green grass, just a few steps away from the execution chamber, contrasts with the hostility of the concrete of the prisons and the steel of the cages. For them, this ultimate pleasure is paradoxically the antechamber to death. Curtis McCarty remembers his release after being cleared: "I'd forgotten how soft the grass was, how slightly padded it felt when you put your foot on it. For 22 years, my feet had been on nothing but concrete. […] For the first few weeks, I couldn't open a door. My parents doubted my mental state. But all my adult life, during 22 years of imprisonment, I was conditioned. As soon as I got to a door, I had to stop and wait for a guard to open it for me. The reflex of having had my hands tied for so long, of never having been free to go through a door, to open it myself, remained in my memory. I had to make a conscious effort to readjust. My mother laughed at me, I stupidly waited for her to open the door for me before going into a store, I didn't dare go through on my own, instinctively, like an animal forbidden to cross a boundary."

Some cells are closed by a barred door, allowing communication with other inmates on death row, and even exchanges of objects, using a string that can be transferred from one cell to another. Others are closed by a solid door fitted with a half-height system for passing meal trays. The whole system is a vicious circle. Oppressed as they are, convicts have no other means of resistance than to insert themselves into the slightest loophole in the system, whenever it exists. In this institution governed by excess, the response of this population denied

---

149. Kevin Cooper, 54, locked up for 24 years at San Quentin prison, San Francisco, California.

all humanity, on the rare occasions when it can express itself, either individually or collectively through riots, has no other vector than excess or violence. This is just enough to justify in the eyes of public opinion that these individuals are monsters who urgently need to be further oppressed.

Minimum food requirements for survival

Death row inmates are unanimous in their complaints about the meals served on death row. Even more than a reproach against a cuisine that is not to the taste of the majority, two essential points are particularly evocative, firstly of the state of public finances in the United States, and secondly of the underlying mentality, making death row inmates with no future whatsoever, individuals on whom the State invests nothing. From the point of view of the quantity and variety of meals served, even if here again there are disparities among the 34 states that still maintain capital punishment in 2011, the economic crisis is bringing food conditions in some US states dangerously close to those observed in Burundi, where a similar survey was carried out in 2007[150]. "You can find anything in the food. Razor blades... the food is crap. I only eat 10% of what they give me. Everything is dirty, including the tray. They let us cook what we can buy, but we have to fiddle with the kettle to heat it up," says A. R. Quantities have become insufficient, quality is mediocre and food is repetitive. States encourage incarceration as an industry with a thriving economy, but no longer have the money to feed prisoners. Before cutting children's school hours, as is starting to happen in California, financiers are reducing prisoners' food portions. "It's pretty much the same meal every day. Except sometimes on Thursdays, we have chicken. [...] In the bowls we find everything, rocks, insects. It sounds inhuman, but I have to eat to keep from starving."[151] Others admit that in other times, they

---

150. GAILLARD (Arnaud), "La peine capitale au Burundi", in *La Peine de mort dans la région des Grands Lacs*, Paris, ECPM, 2007.

151. T. P., 25, Mississippi death row, interview conducted in July 2010.

wouldn't even have given their dogs this crushed food in the form of porridge! For several years now, as a cost-cutting measure, some states have been providing death row inmates with just two meals a day, and no hot meals at all on weekends. In Tennessee, on the other hand, the food seems more respectable. With humor, A. R. explains: "I call it 747 food. It's only subsistence food, but it's not enough." For those lucky enough to receive a little money from the outside, there is, as everywhere, the possibility of improving daily life with three-dollar seasonings or fruit.

Time reference points between inside and outside are completely disrupted. Breakfast is often served around 6am. In Texas, to save on guard rotas, breakfast is served at 3am, lunch at 10am and dinner at 3pm. Unlike conventional imprisonment, convicts eat alone in their cells, on canteen trays. Meals are only a daily episode in the "survival" of caged individuals, and the time difference between life on the outside and life on the inside underscores the break between the life beyond the walls and the lives imposed on death row. These are bodies to be filled, organs to be nourished, so that this physiological entity can function until the day when justice decides to proceed with the killing. Behind this function of feeding, of filling, almost according to industrial methods, there is no notion of pleasure. We remain in the realm of pure animality, echoing the social representation of death row inmates in the United States.

Sleep patterns are also disrupted. For safety reasons, and to ensure that death row is watertight, death row inmates are required at regular intervals to indicate their presence and survival. This is the counting procedure, which takes place night and day, as another aspect of continuous surveillance. The aim is to ensure that no one has escaped, that everyone is in their place, but also that everyone is alive in a world where suicide is forbidden. Depending on the level of surveillance that determines the incarceration regime, between those who are granted prerogatives and those who are punished with more constraints, everyone is disturbed not only during the day, but also at night, by the supervisors' scheduled rounds. On Texas death row, renowned for its extreme severity, every four hours, guards knock on the doors of convicts on level 1, look through the eyepiece and demand that everyone identify themselves by name, prison number and prison ID card. On level 2, these checks are carried out every hour and a half. On level 3, death row inmates are checked every 45 minutes, day and night, without respite. Prison management is determined to establish meticulous, obsessive control over every material, temporal and existential detail, so as to imprint in the minds of inmates that, with the exception of the content of their thoughts, absolutely everything is controlled by a prison authority that interferes to the point of dispossessing individuals of their autonomy as living beings. The protocol is pushed to excess during the *"death watch"* phase, i.e. the confinement in a special unit prior to execution. Not only is the last nights' sleep interrupted every 45 minutes, but prison management also takes the liberty of using cameras to film the cell in which the condemned man lives out his final hours alone, 24 hours a day. With a blatant disregard for the dignity of the men and women locked up, the will of the total institution relentlessly scrutinizes its prey with the aim of triumphing over total control of the individuals held in respect. These coercive practices imprint the penal institution's will to dominate on the minds of those condemned to death, a will to total control that echoes an ambition for infallibility. The supremacy of penitentiary authority stems from this demand, but so too does the feeling that death row inmates are plunged into a never-ending hell, an existence that liquefies into a feeling of total confusion, anguish and hostility.

The derisory interest in the health of those who are about to die

For the same reasons as with food, the state invests nothing in the health of those it plans to kill. It doesn't matter if there are appeals pending that could lead to a future release. There is a sense of fragmentation in the minds of those condemned to death: "You lose a little bit of your health every day."[152] Serious illnesses receive little treatment, examinations are only carried out as a last resort, and each condemned prisoner has to fight to have his or her pathologies taken into account. A. R. complains that "it's never the same drugs. Nothing is adapted, so many prisoners die here". Gloria Goodwin-Killian recalls: "The care is so bad that the administration has admitted that they kill people through medical error quite regularly. People die from nothing in prison, just because they're misdiagnosed, mistreated. You can die from asthma, from a simple abscess that degenerates, and with the crisis it gets worse." Here again, depending on the state and the prison warden, the situation can be better or worse. Women are subjected to the same regime, motivated by the same circumstances. Curtis McCarty recalls the conditions in Oklahoma: "They did the minimum to keep us alive. But they didn't treat cancer or heart attacks, there was no medication for HIV. There was no compassion, they didn't treat, they didn't try to bring the family closer together. It's even forbidden to donate our organs." Mumia Abu-Jamal remembers one of his fellow inmates: "The doctors didn't tell him he had cancer, because they didn't want to spend money to treat him, knowing he was sentenced to death. The guy figured it out on his own and preferred to hang himself, because he didn't want to have to endure the suffering without any painkillers. He knew very well the excruciating pain that cancer causes towards the end." As for Sandrine Ageorges-Skinner, she recalls that her husband, incarcerated on Polunsky's death row in Texas, had to go to court to obtain treatment for hepatitis C, contracted through the use of non-disinfected razors randomly distributed by the prison administration. It took three years of litigation to finally obtain the cheapest and least effective treatment. Similarly, in Texas, for a death row inmate to obtain anti-depressants, he or she must confess suicidal desires to a psychiatrist, or be diagnosed as psychotic. In both cases, there is a corollary risk of permanently affecting the legitimacy of appeals. Mental health and

---

152. T. P., 25, death row, Parchman, Mississippi.

well-being thus become objects of blackmail, in competition with the constitutional right to defend oneself.

Yet, ironically, because execution is a mission that must be accomplished, suicides are prevented. They are seen as a metaphorical escape, contradicting the authority of the judicial decision. Death must take place in a court of law, according to the terms of the law, following a protocol specific to each state. However, it is inevitable that suicidal thoughts cross the minds of death row inmates, who have no other horizon than the interminable wait for appeals, appeal procedures and the hopes placed in the project of a new trial. Cliff Johnson, a lawyer in Jackson, Mississippi, remembers his client: "After all his appeals, Bobby was suffering from depression, he was suffering from daily life on death row, the cramped conditions of his cell, the lack of air conditioning... He couldn't sleep because of the heat, and when he came back from the shower soaking wet, he would beg to be able to sleep at last. He couldn't take it any more - I can understand that, and so can everyone else, given the 24 years he'd spent locked up on death row and the miserable life he'd led since childhood. I tried very hard to convince him that he had to live, but it was hard to find any meaning in going on living. So he gave up the pursuit of his last resort, and asked to be executed. The State agreed. This decision was irreversible: they call them "volunteers". In fact, Bobby's case became a real story, as to whether the State should satisfy him, i.e. commit suicide... [...] Still, when Bobby wanted to go back on his decision, not die and try again to resume his appeal, they refused. So they executed him just as he was getting his taste for life back... All my life I'll be thinking of him from now on."

The contradictory situation of making individuals survive, sometimes against their will, in order to be able to carry out a legal decision, produces the most ubiquitous behaviors. Curtis McCarty recounts how, at McAlester prison in Oklahoma, a death row inmate, R. McK., refused to leave his life in the hands of the prison administration, choosing to commit suicide on the morning of his execution. Found in an apparent coma, the guards refused to save him, thinking it was a ruse to escape. For hours, they let him die, convinced it was a feint. When they realized that the coma was deep enough to be fatal, they rushed him to hospital that afternoon to resuscitate him so they could execute him that evening. He concludes by saying, "This is the most incredible thing I've ever experienced in my life!"

In the same way, and because the ineptitude of the death penalty has many faces, since smoking is now banned in most American prisons, death row inmates are deprived of this pleasure until their execution, on the pretext that cigarettes, being bad for your health, must be banned from all prison premises. A. R. says: "You can't smoke! I have a heart condition, I know it's not advisable, but I love it and they won't let me have it, when in the end they want to kill me anyway. It's completely absurd!" Among last wishes, that of smoking a final cigarette is now the stuff of legend and history. The same regime applies to alcohol. The deprivation of pleasures is total and definitive, and carries with it a moral injunction that nothing can deflect, not even the death to come within the hour.

Resistance is not death

More than any other form of imprisonment, the death sentence causes social death for those around the condemned. For example, never receiving a visit while locked up and awaiting death is the ordeal of many a recluse. There are two categories of condemned inmates on death row. Those in total obscurity, the poorest and most numerous, with no family and no lawyer worthy of the name, are sometimes executed even before all their appeals have been exhausted[153]. They are regarded by society as second-class beings. Their fate is consigned

---

153. Several death row inmates in Texas were executed when their federal appeals were rejected, either because their attorneys had missed the deadline or because they had filed appeals whose elements were incompatible with habeas corpus standards.

to the modesty of prison cemeteries, with a cross or plaque indicating the surname, first name and date of death, whether by execution or so-called "natural" death, the direct consequence of the endless wear and tear of a lifelong incarceration with no horizon whatsoever. In Texas, the number engraved on the cement cross will begin with 999[154].

Then there are those, guilty or innocent, whose cases are sufficiently contentious to fuel external mobilization. Some of these are represented by a lawyer who is more effective than at their first trial, backed up by a support committee, visitors and correspondents. For some, the support is moderately, if not widely, publicized. All have to endure their fate under the same conditions, but some are lucky enough to stay alive, as long as some of them are on the outside. In all cases, the torture is obvious. It causes social, physical and mental damage inversely proportional to the strength of character of each individual. With an acuity similar to that of the terminally ill, many death row inmates in the United States have to wake up every day with a heightened awareness of their finitude. Belonging more to the second group, the condemned prisoners interviewed all showed themselves to be extremely in control of their existence, demonstrating an exponential imagination to activate internal or external levers, to generate compensations, like living beings consciously on borrowed time, never resigned to the submission of a barbaric, useless and unjust system, from which they draw an anger that is sometimes energizing, sometimes desperate. E. M. confesses: "I meditate on positive things, and try to think about the future." M. adds: "I just try to keep my mind in a state, to make things better. I don't need much to be happy. I force myself not to think about certain things, and in the end, I'm not afraid of anything… Except snakes!"

---

154. From 1924 (before then, the PA management didn't deal with executions, that was the role of the county sheriff) to the 1960s, on the graves, there was the name and a date of death with an *X* to specify "death by execution". From then on, there was only the case number, accompanied by the date of execution and an *X*.

Despite the courage required to remain on their feet in these conditions of confinement, despite the responsibility of the guilty and the rage of the innocent, those condemned to death must find outlets to find meaning in an existence that is drained, wrung out, controlled and hampered on all sides. Kevin Cooper, incarcerated in San Quentin, California, where living conditions are more appreciable, still hopes that his innocence will one day be proven. In the meantime, he organizes basketball tournaments. And should things ever go wrong for him, he says: "It's a never-ending hell here. I find it hard to let them have the power to kill me. If they program my death, if they think they have the power to kill me, then maybe I'd rather choose death myself, and beat them to it."

As most possessions are forbidden in the cells, tightly controlled by regulations that, more often than not, only get tougher, you have to use a lot of imagination to replace what's missing. Take, for example, the world-famous case of death row inmate Caryl Chessman, who became a best-selling author behind bars. When the prison administration tried to prevent him from writing on paper, he used toilet paper. He managed to get a second book published by passing around pages signed with his fingerprints, unbeknownst to the guards. In 1959, the Supreme Court[155] questioned the penitentiary administration's relentless refusal to allow him to do anything. In the end, the judges concluded that these prohibitions amounted to totalitarianism. Even today, death row inmates have to develop unparalleled ingenuity to make matter out of paper pulp, make fire with electric batteries and metalized strips from the inside of Tetra Pak cans, make paintbrushes out of hair, make music with their mouths. No one is allowed to own anything on death row, apart from a few quota books from the prison bookshop, a transparent clock radio to monitor what might be lurking there, a television and sometimes a typewriter, paper and pencils, the minimum toiletries and underwear. These conditions vary according

---

155. "Chessman v. Teets," 354 U.S. 156 (June 10, 1957).

to the state[156], and the disciplinary status of death row inmates. E. M. describes his daily life as follows: "I read fitness magazines, romance novels and books on psychology. You're not allowed to have more than three books in your cell. It's also impossible to look at your body. There are few or no mirrors. And when we leave the cell, it's to enter another one, the walk-in cell, which is barely bigger, where we can't be more than three people. We've been like caged lions for years."

After several years, when death row inmates reach a rank justified by their exemplary behavior on death row, in some states the administration grants them a professional occupation[157], sometimes paid a few *cents an* hour. In other states, the work is compulsory, unpaid and carried out under difficult conditions. This is the case, for example, in the Southern states, where death row inmates must work in scorching heat reminiscent of the hard labor of the old prison camps. Symbolically, these missions give meaning to this reconstituted micro-society. Mumia Abu-Jamal, incarcerated for 29 years in Pittsburgh, Pennsylvania, is an extremely erudite man. A former journalist and writer, he continues to write and publish with a particular acuity when it comes to talking about his country, politics and the workings of society, on a national or global scale. In contrast to his intellectual abilities, he has become a soda delivery boy at the school. As he explains in a factual way, devoid of humility or pride, this activity is beneficial to him: "I work as a *'sodaman'* until September. Every two weeks, we can buy coca. It's a great job, it gives pleasure to people who haven't had a coke in years, and it allows me to wander around the establishment and create social links, discovering who I am with. Otherwise, I shovel snow in winter."

All prisoners are dressed in loose-fitting outfits whose color changes according to the state, like convicts of yesteryear. Even singularity of dress is made impossible in this total institution, which has power over

---

156. Texas is the only state to ban televisions on death row.
157. This option is not available in all states.

everything, decides everything, levels and reduces existences. Gender distinctions are denied, as Gloria Goodwin-Killian explains: "We're dressed in men's prison garb, clothes that are too long. Jewelry is forbidden, except for a vague religious pendant. Perfume and make-up were also banned for security reasons. Every year it got stricter. The mirrors were set so high, as if for men, that for years I could only see the top of my hair in the mirror." Whether it's freedom, recognition, justice, emotion or perspective, death row in the U.S. organizes a life of emptiness, elaborates nothingness under control, and does nothing but maintain in a sketchy existence those whom justice waits impatiently to kill. In a climate of paranoia pushed to the limit, because everything is forbidden, because the rules level all individuals at the most restrictive denominator, even death row inmates who, for 29 years, have demonstrated their discipline and submission to their incarcerated status, are denied musical instruments. Mumia Abu-Jamal recounts how his life has changed since one of his visitors taught him music in the visiting room, through Plexiglas and without any accessories. He demonstrates survival through total asceticism: "Instruments are forbidden, so I drew a keyboard on paper and the sound is in my head. It's one of the most incredible experiences of my life. It taught me how to write and read music. On Tuesdays, I do it with my teacher, and during the week I write a little opera. It's transformed my life. I write in my head, and another prisoner taught me how to write music. In fact, I've always been an artist, and they're not going to stop me staying one!"

The painful after-effects of security issues

It's important to understand that the death sentence is not limited to the execution itself, but is embodied in all the parameters of the experience of confinement that prison administrations organize to better destructure individuals. In the majority of death rows, it's not a question of life, but rather of survival, of a perpetual struggle against the madness that inevitably afflicts some, against the daily humiliations and everything that the penal system has put in place to reduce the living to a mechanic of organs drowned in a hostile environment.

And even if the common areas of these recently dehumanizing prisons resemble aseptic hospitals, with their shiny, freshly-painted corridors, the cells are more often than not dilapidated. They bear the scars of the pain, and sometimes the madness, of those who, by being locked up like animals for so many years, have lost all sense of time and basic hygiene. In this prison hell, some regress to such a stage that they end up embodying what the outside majority tries to project with certainty, a majority intimately convinced that death row inmates are monsters and sub-humans.

As in all prison systems, a proportion of guards behave with humanity and respect towards the people in their care. Others, on the other hand, develop sadistic practices, playing with the prospect of death, and distilling daily humiliations for these convicts who have no other social relations than to meet their jailers. And if, according to the inmates, excesses are frequent, the prison administration is generally above the law. The actions of prison staff are rarely prosecuted, and conditions of confinement are exceptionally recognized as illegal by the courts. A case in point is that of a complaint of ill-treatment, which took almost 30 years to investigate, initiated by an inmate, David Ruiz[158]. A judge finally ruled that Texas prisons were unconstitutional, and that incarceration under these conditions constituted cruel and unusual treatment. David Ruiz nevertheless ended his life in solitary confinement. Granting prerogatives to death row inmates, recognizing them as victims, contradicts the culture of punishment that is particularly widespread in the southern states. All the requests expressed by death row inmates, and by extension the entire criminal procedure, operate on the basis of a balance of power based on attrition. In order not to be discouraged by this war of nerves that governs and interferes in the slightest dissatisfactions maintained like so much sadism, maintaining one's morale requires the most solid mental

---

158. "Sick in secret: The hidden world of prison health care. A squeaky wheel who's been heard for three decades", *The Statesman*, Austin, Texas.

structure. The strongest resist, while the weakest plunge and regress, subject to a form of prison Darwinism in which confinement artificially organizes a selection of individuals capable of surviving intact. Often, only external support, whether individual or collectivized by national or international campaigns, as well as the hope of future legal recourse, enables the physical and mental integrity of the self to be maintained, as an identified course on a horizon that is nevertheless always uncertain.

For budgetary reasons, human resources are gradually being replaced by a battery of cameras, allowing us to punish the guards as much as the convicts. This also prevents all the little adjustments to the rules, such as bartering and other internal trades, which used to make life a little more comfortable, while maintaining a semblance of social relations. Year after year, death row and prisons as a whole justify their characterization as total institutions, denying all aspects of the humanity of those locked up. Thus envisaged, American incarceration goes beyond the panoptic conception, omitting any pedagogical vocation, with the desire to add ever more coercion to the guarding of these individuals destined to be killed.

In line with the same objective of security, and in order not to contradict the reputation of maximum-security prisons, even the recreation and exercise areas are to prevent gatherings, thus avoiding the numerous riots that have punctuated the history of American incarceration. Mumia Abu-Jamal explains: "There's a desire to limit encounters to avoid riots. Before, there were seven cages in the yard, with five men in each one. Now there are 15 smaller cages, with a maximum of two people inside." Excessive isolation and the introduction of permanent control processes are justified by the desire to neutralize the formation of groups and gangs, regardless of whether this degree of inhumanity generates extreme behavior likely to transform, one day, into new forms of general rebellion. A. R. analyzes daily life as follows: "Everyone has to be separated at all times. Every little thing can take on major proportions in prison. It's a world of savages. Even a joke can result in six months' disciplinary punishment. A terrible revenge can get you killed. Many here are mentally ill. Others have nothing to lose; they're already criminals condemned to die, so…". This is the ambiguity of the death penalty. The desire to subjugate individuals who are regarded as monsters, and who are kept on probation pending a judicial decision that could confirm the sentence, is tantamount to training wild animals. It takes an enormous amount of willpower to maintain a sense of dignity in these conditions, without which the prison administration finds itself faced with criminals whom the legal system has transformed into savages who are difficult, if not illusory, to control. It is the circumstances of domination and the absence of hope that transform these beings into indomitable individuals to be wary of, or that accentuate the already often severe mental pathologies omnipresent in prison establishments.

Sociability is severely curtailed, and daily life is regulated in such a way that at no time can inmates become a decisive, active mass that the guards cannot control. Here again, security conditions take precedence over the humanity of the detainees. Gloria Goodwin-Killian remembers: "When the general alarm sounded, often for nothing at all, we all had to sit on the floor immediately, to prevent us from becoming violent. And we had better obey, like animals. This procedure may be appropriate for men, but we women are neither violent nor dangerous against the prison administration." This economy in the management of beings is inherent in any constraint that pits numbers, in this case inmates, against constraint. A. R. describes the courtyard in which he is allowed to spend a maximum of one hour a day, to escape the solitude of his cell: "There can be four of us in the courtyard, where we have nothing to do but walk! It's wired like a cage." Mumia Abu-Jamal points out that "there's often no walk for seven days for one reason or another. So we stay 24 hours a day in our cells, without explanation. In any case, we can't rebel."

In Tennessee, again, conditions are more enviable. A. R. explains: "In the yard, there are three small cages, with six people in each. We can play cards, handball or basketball." For W. M., "the advantage of going out in the yard for an hour a day is to get fresh air, to be outside, despite the bars everywhere, to run around a bit, even if it's very small, and to see the sky and the sun. Sometimes we talk together too".

In some cases, the cells are closed with doors made of openwork bars, allowing continuous surveillance on death row. This system allows objects to be exchanged by means of a string that can be transferred from one *cage to* another. Other cells are enclosed by a solid door with a trapdoor halfway up and an eyecup. This closed *cage*, inhabited all day long, resembles a coffin in which death row inmates feel they are walled up alive. Through these doors, the inmates talk to each other, without ever seeing each other, in a complete cacophony where each one has to pick out the phrases that concern him or her in order to reconstitute a semblance of conversation, in any case collective. This noisy atmosphere, in which the respective distresses are expressed, is reminiscent of the aggressive hubbub of the worst asylums, where daily life becomes surreal, as witnessed by W. M., an inmate on death row in Parchman, Mississippi, when he reports this discussion: "Today is my last visit, I'm going to be executed in three days, and you?"

The rest of the sociability takes place in relationships with the guards, who restrain the hands to get to the shower or visiting room, and serve meals through a small trapdoor in the cell, or under the bars of the open door. Behind the lack of ordinary social relations, A. R., a prisoner in Mississippi, expresses his lack of tenderness, an elementary, almost gregarious tenderness, devoid of feeling: "The first time a guard touched me on death row, saying 'How you doing, man?', it was delicious to finally have contact with a human being. It's impossible to compensate for tenderness, you stay focused on yourself and survive." Relations with the guards are generally described as fairly decent, with no violence: "They do their job, even if it's a dirty job."[159] Others, however, have more painful memories: "They don't want to get involved. Last year, a guy was stabbed six times in the prison, but the guards didn't do anything, they didn't dare move." Despite this violence intrinsic to punitive confinement, E. M. concludes: "I'm not afraid of others here, if not of the court and the judges. They're the most dangerous people here. I'm afraid of the judicial system in general. They have the power to do what they want, it's power more than justice. They're the most powerful."

When outside meets inside

"I come with stories that make people laugh, he needs to laugh," says this mother of a condemned man who moved to be closer to her only son's final resting place: "And when I pass by the prison on my way back from shopping, I honk my horn continuously in the distance on the road, with the hope that he'll know it's me and that I'm thinking of him. The prison guards must think I'm crazy, but I don't care, I'm driving so they can't stop me." What's left to maintain relationships beyond the glassed-in visiting rooms for years on end? The death penalty is not only a means of torturing prisoners, it is also a torment for their loved ones. What can we say about this woman who has only her brother left on death row? What can we say about the mother who has dedicated her life to ensuring the survival of her only son in the dungeons of the 21st century? What can we say about these children who will soon lose their mother or father, never to be able to touch them again[160], except in the minutes following the execution, when the skin is still warm, before the body cools completely? Golda wonders: "Why does

---

159. T.P., 25, Parchman, Mississippi.

160. In many states, prison management does not allow the family of the condemned prisoner to spend moments or hours with him or her without a separation device, free in a room to touch, talk to and hug each other. Relatives are not allowed to approach the body they have not touched since entering death row until after death. In Tennessee, among others, as well as in Louisiana and Mississippi, a small windowless room allows the family to gather around the condemned man a few hours before the execution.

the state of Texas continue to impose this torture? Other states allow contact visits, but here it's still impossible. I'll never be able to touch my son again." What's being said over there is that not even China dares this torture. This suffering is unknown to the general public. Blindly, they are supposed to redeem the crime committed, in a process that would cancel out by compensation the suffering of the murdered person's loved ones. This illusion carries with it a symbolic dimension that satisfies even the most educated retentionist consciences.

In the visiting rooms of most prisons, death row inmates are separated from the outside world by an armored pane of glass, through which no physical contact is possible, not even a caress. How else are we to say goodbye, if not by ignoring this imaginary wall, symbolically touching the glass in the same place, each on his own side? The confinement of one against the freedom of the other. Death row in the United States is designed to create a radical separation between inside and outside. Only the voice, the gaze and the image of a bust surmounted by a head can pass through. This dehumanizing principle, which has become almost familiar in fiction from the United States, remains a shocking and unusual situation when confronted. To be so close and yet unable to touch or feel each other. There is something contrary to the natural order in this security provision, which poorly conceals the "sadism" of its punitive value, in the words of Golda, who has been forbidden to touch her son for 15 years. Even so, she says: "If the worst comes to the worst, I won't go to the execution; I don't want to watch them kill my son. His father will go, he knows he won't be alone, I'll be in the next town, but I won't be able to watch."

In Texas, apart from communications with their lawyers, condemned prisoners are only entitled to one 5-minute phone call every 90 days. This provision is not respected by the new director of the Polunsky Unit in Texas, whose managerial and security visions seem, in the words of death row inmates and their families, very clearly nourished by a desire to destroy the individuals in his care. Everything is done to hamper the ability of death row inmates to support their defense: even lawyers have to file a request for an appeal 24 hours in advance. How can we rationally and technically analyze this restriction in the United States[161]? In Mississippi, E. M. explains, "We can make calls to anyone on our list, which can change every 6 months and contains 10 names." In all cases, calls are recorded, letters are read, and packages are usually forbidden. In some states, as a souvenir, for a few dollars, a guard takes a photo of the condemned man and his visitors. These are the only images that emerge from this world apart, from behind the sharp steel and hostile concrete.

Despite this repetitive aspect of imposed formalism, visits to the visiting room remain for women, mothers and children in general, a rendezvous for which one prepares. Make-up, choice of clothes, perfume: in this moment when the infinite inside meets the so distant outside, it is necessary to transmit an idealized image, to be accomplices around aesthetic and sensual pleasures. It's as much a gift that these generous, faithful women want to modestly entrust to death row inmates, as a discreet desire to maintain an idea of the outside, like a suspended memory, whose timelessness they strive to preserve. These coquetries are both an image of affection and resistance. And yet, even if odors do not penetrate through the armored glass of the visiting rooms, perfume is one of the residual symbolic acts in this existence of imposed withdrawal from the other.

Paradoxically, even though detention on death row constitutes a fatal and definitive break with life on the outside, death row inmates

---

161. In contrast, on California's San Quentin death row, which is home to the largest number of death row inmates, inmates have access to a cell phone for two hours a day to call whoever they wish on collect. The list of visitors is unlimited and can be modified at any time. Visits are made in a cubicle with no separating device, and death row inmates can receive a parcel four times a year, containing clothing, books and food. In their cells, prisoners are free to dress as they please. Prison uniforms are compulsory only outside cells.

frequently mention their own wish not to receive visits. T., an inmate at Parchman, Mississippi, explains: "I prefer not to have visitors. We're treated like animals here, and I don't want to be seen like that. It's too humiliating. W., who is locked up in Mississippi, explains: "I try not to have visitors, I prefer not to let my family see me. I don't want them to see me in chains." Curtis McCarty, on the contrary, remembers surviving thanks to his parents' support: "My parents have never missed a visiting room in 22 years, despite my mother's illness." His father recalls, "We went every month, and every time we thought, 'Are they going to kill our son next month?' My wife was getting sicker and sicker, but she insisted on going. Over there, we were considered less than nothing. Sometimes we were even humiliated. [...] The day he was released was the happiest day of our lives." This is the stigma by contagion expressed by Erving Goffman[162], which Jessica Mederson, *pro bono* lawyer for a death row inmate, describes thus, recounting her surprise when she took on the case of Michael Perry, finally executed at 26 in Huntsville, Texas: "In civil cases, you get the same consideration in both cases, no matter which side of the case you represent. Whereas in criminal cases, we only represent a guilty party, and I was shocked to see how poorly we were regarded. Yet in criminal cases, it's not just about money, it's about human life, so it's more serious."

Justice is so authoritarian that no leniency is shown in the details of its application. The person who is to be killed has no rights, since he is denied even the right to live. His family suffers the same humiliation, as they carry the murderer's blood within them. When Jessica Mederson, Michael Perry's lawyer, asks the judge to postpone the execution on the grounds that her mother is already mourning the death of her own husband, Michael's father, and that two such close bereavements could be fatal to her, the judge's reply is unambiguous: "Why wait? The only

---

162. GOFFMAN (Erving), *Stigmate, les usages sociaux des handicaps*, Paris, Éditions de Minuit, coll. "Le Sens commun", 1975.

legitimate mourning is that of the murder victim's family. The family of the executed man has only a secondary mourning, so the execution date will not be postponed."

Chapter 9:
Execution

History has already witnessed the effectiveness of the professional network that allows, at the heart of an institution, through written and often legal motivations, supported by an ideology in a position of strength, to have tasks carried out that an elementary morality, common to our species, repudiates at the very heart of consciences. Whatever the past of the executed, the mission of these protean executioners remains the killing of a human being. There is a minute before and a minute after. There's the passing of life, and then the silence of an uninhabited body, a frozen smile, cooling skin, stiffening limbs and a face violently poisoned by the lethal injection. There's the hot breath and the icy atmosphere. None of the directors in charge of executions can find compassionate ears to express these emotions, of which they are both witnesses and sometimes unwitting actors. They are part of a duty inherent in their function.

Killing is perceived as ambivalent. It is at once an act detached from the sentence, since the executor of the "dirty deeds" is not the person who condemned him. It is the tragic staging of the will of judges, prosecutors and juries, of a society that demands vengeance and believes itself protected by the death of others. They are also ordinary minutes, in all their regulatory and technical aspects. On the day of an execution, Curtis McCarty recounts: "You feel a sense of solidarity with the person who's about to be killed and whom you've come to know. So we all tap the metal of the toilet with our shoe just before the execution, just to let him know that we're there, that we haven't forgotten him. It can go on for quite a long time, and it's obviously very noisy because it echoes around the establishment. Then we stop to give him a little peace and quiet, the chance to die with dignity, in silence. It's not so much a way of protesting against the execution - we don't have the power to do that - it's just a way of saying: we're here, we know what you're doing, we're not turning a blind eye to the fact that you're going to kill one of our own."

The torture of waiting

And as if to add to the torture, sometimes, just moments before the fateful hour, the authorities order a stay of execution, even though the morbid staging has already begun. To die or not to die? We have to imagine the psychological consequences of this perverse game with the nerves of the condemned man, his family and his lawyers. Try to imagine what the nights and days that follow are like, after the trauma of a programmed and then deprogrammed death. This lack of respect for the anguish of dying is the affirmation of a ruthless power, embodied by an all-powerful judicial mechanism, capable of killing or pardoning at will. This is the prerogative of assassins. It takes an impressive mental structure to escape the madness of this moment, which sometimes repeats itself. Mumia Abu-Jamal was twice taken to the execution chamber, only to have his sentence suspended. Kevin Cooper in California, Abu-Ali Abdur Rahman in Tennessee and Hank Skinner in Texas also saw their respective executions stayed on several occasions, just hours before the fateful moment. Although it constitutes a stay of execution, this frequent practice is experienced as an insult, a traumatizing humiliation, emanating from a judicial administration whose organization is decidedly sadistic.

International bodies are also looking into the torture mechanism of waiting for death, which varies greatly from country to country.

Some are quicker than others. The average time between conviction and execution is 12 years in the United States. Since the enactment of the AEDPA in 1996[163], this period has tended to be reduced to five or six years for those sentenced after that date. International rules say that this wait is too long, that it constitutes torture in itself. However, the United States refuses to follow these observations. The judicial process, including appeals and the inertia of the system before execution, is particularly long in California. The average length of incarceration on death row is between 20 and 24 years. Steven F. Shatz, Professor of Criminology at the University of San Francisco, points out that "internationally, waiting to die for such a long time is considered torture by human rights defenders and the European Court of Human Rights". He cites the case of "Soering v. United Kingdom"[164] in which the refusal of extradition to the United States "was not merely the application of the punishment prescribed by law [the death sentence, *NDA*], but rather his immersion in the phenomenon of death row, where he would be held for an unknown period, awaiting execution. The European Court of Human Rights has demanded that no extradition should take place pending a decision on this issue". However, because the U.S. Supreme Court has refused to consider this parameter, it is difficult to counter this argument as much as it is to define the length of time from which we can speak of torture.

Technicizing killing to kill cleanly and humanely

The debate is often centered on the method of execution, which must obey the ambition to improve "good death techniques". The desire to master the act of killing calls for the use of a tool, instruments that put

---

163. Reminder: Anti-Terrorism and Effective Death Penalty Act (AEDPA) of 1996 (Clinton administration).

164. "Soering v. United Kingdom" 11 Eur. Ct. H.R. (ser. A) (1989) is a major case law of the European Court of Human Rights (ECHR), establishing that the extradition of a young German national to the United States to face death penalty charges violated article 3 of the European Convention on Human Rights (ECHR), which guarantees the right to protection from inhuman and degrading treatment.

distance between the human hand, directly representing justice, and the act of killing. The aim is to execute without giving the impression of murder. Above all, it's a question of making the task of the executioners, who aren't even called that, easier. From century to century, techniques have varied and become more technical. France commissioned a doctor to invent the guillotine. A little later, the Americans invented the electric chair: giving death by energy, mastering electricity to commit a clean crime, without bloodshed, with a scientific seriousness that neither hanging nor poisoning offer. Steven F. Shatz, a professor of criminology, writes of his country: "The history has always been to try to kill people 'pleasantly', but every time it's painful, whether it's by firing squad or hanging. But this country always wants to be at the cutting edge of progress, so as soon as it's part of a scientific, technical operation, then it gives the impression of progress." Thus, as the successor to hanging, the electric chair, the principal method of execution between 1924 and 1964, was included in the cultural landscape of the United States. Often, the population gave it a "little name", denoting a kind of emotional relationship tinged with irony. In Texas, people called her "Old Sparky"[165]. Elsewhere, other names were given, such as "Sizzlin' Sally", "Old Smokey", "Yellow Mama"[166], "Gruesome Gertie"[167], etc. These names represent the personification of an object that does the "dirty work" for the executioner. With electrocution, it's as if technology is erasing the human hand. There's a desire to externalize the execution while retaining an incarnate form, halfway between thing and being, for this object identified with the justice of a state, on which hundreds of people *were grilled in a* sort of collective self-da-fé. Even today, although electric chairs are less widely used than lethal injection, they still belong to a form of the past that can be visited, commented on and exhibited in prisons or museums for

---

165. The nickname was also used in Florida, Georgia, Illinois, Kentucky, Louisiana, Ohio, Oklahoma, New York and Virginia.
166. "Yellow Mama".
167. "Appalling Gertie".

adults or schoolchildren[168]. They are not yet the remnants of a bygone aberration, yet this is undoubtedly the fate in store for future generations, who will see in this killing tool the barbaric errors of a society that is still contemporary. The U.S. administration long ago realized the limitations of this electrical device, as Professor Shatz explains: "People realized that electric chairs were random, and people died directly or were roasted on the spot. So we used gas chambers[169], because with gas, it's progressive and therefore more humane."

So, before gas chambers were discovered in Nazi extermination camps, the USA had already begun executing in these airtight alcoves from 1924 onwards. Today, five states[170] still have the option of using the gas chamber as an alternative to lethal injection, which has become the new modern means of clean execution. The gas used in some states, including Arizona, was Zyklon B, the same as that used in the industrialization of death organized by the Third Reich. As Professor Rick Halperin explains: "No one wants to be lumped in with the Nazis. Everyone agrees that it was the worst regime Humanity has ever known." This is one of the reasons why American gas chambers, often designed to execute two people at the same time if necessary, were abandoned as the main killing device, as Prof. Shatz testifies: "It seemed like progress until we knew how it was used and how many people died that way under Hitler's Reich. So the reputation of the gas chambers was sullied."

---

168. In Nashville, Tennessee, schoolchildren can visit the *death* chamber and the entire execution unit. On a regular basis, the prison warden welcomes entire classes, who come to see the killing process in a cold and explained way. The information received is not, however, information that can be criticized or criticized. It's a passive awareness.

169. Eleven people have been executed in gas chambers since executions resumed in 1976. Walter LaGrand was the last person executed in a gas chamber in Arizona in 1999.

170. Arizona, California, Maryland, Missouri, Wyoming.

Since the resumption of executions in 1977[171], the new technique that has triumphed in the United States is lethal injection. This is in response to constitutional imperatives, which admit the possibility of death in the name of justice, but outlaw unnecessary suffering. It is on the basis of this argument that lethal injection and the written protocols that govern the process, when they exist, are regularly called into question. Here again, the history of American executions intersects with that of Nazi Germany, as Rick Halperin points out that lethal injection was invented by Karl Brandt, Hitler's personal physician, to put 10,000 defective children to death. He adds: "The technique was primarily designed to make the killing easier for those who were to carry it out. Prof. Shatz adds: "When we accept the idea of the death penalty, we also accept that the State has an obligation to ensure that there is no suffering, which is unnecessary and unconstitutional. [...] But with lethal injection, we can see condemned prisoners suffocating for 6 minutes, 8 minutes, 10 minutes, 12 minutes, sometimes much longer. It's an unbearable spectacle.

---

171. Gary Gilmore is shot in Utah after a 10-year moratorium on executions between 1967 and 1977.

Summary table of execution methods[172]

Method	Number of executions per method	Number of states authorizing the method	Jurisdictions that authorize
Lethal injection	1,085	34 states + military and federal jurisdiction	Alabama, Arizona, Arkansas, California, North Carolina, South Carolina, Colorado, Connecticut, South Dakota, Delaware, Florida, Georgia, Idaho, Indiana, Kansas, Kentucky, Louisiana, Maryland, Mississippi, Missouri, Montana, Nebraska, Nevada, New Hampshire, Oklahoma, Oregon, Pennsylvania, Tennessee, Texas, Utah, Virginia, Washington**, Wyoming, military and federal jurisdiction.
Electric wheelchair*	157	9	Alabama, Arkansas, Florida, Kentucky, Oklahoma, Tennessee, South Carolina, Virginia
Gas chamber	11	4	Arizona, California, Missouri, Wyoming
Hanging*	3	2	New Hampshire, Washington
Firing squad*	3	1	Oklahoma***, Utah***

* All propose lethal injection as the main method.

** Ohio opted for a single-product lethal injection protocol in November 2009. Washington State made the same choice on March 2, 2010, although convicts can still opt for the three-product protocol.

*** Utah no longer offers firing squad as an option, except for death row inmates who opted for this method before it was abolished. Oklahoma offers firing squad only if lethal injection or the electric chair are deemed unconstitutional.

---

172. Source: "Methods used", summary table, Death Penalty Information Center (www.deathpenaltyinfo.org), updated 2011.

Most states offer two methods of execution. One is old-fashioned (electric chair, firing squad, gas chamber), and the other (lethal injection) *has been democratized* since its first use in Texas in 1982. As time goes by, American legislators are seeking to develop an execution device that is simply a neutral killing, without generating suffering and minimizing the spectacle. As if death could express nothing: no screams, no muscular twitching, no bloodshed. Even today, there's the fantasy of finding a "humane" way to kill the one who has killed, to kill with justice, in a clean, hygienic, scientific, almost medical way, according to a process that is enhanced by technology and therefore unquestionable and harmless in the eyes of the collective conscience. A process which, as it becomes increasingly technicalized, would lose its analogy with blood crimes, those which justice punishes. So, to set ourselves apart from non-democratic, *still savage nations*, in the land of freedom, we would kill in a civilized way. The second drug used in lethal injections is designed to paralyze the condemned man's muscles, so as to render imperceptible any reaction of pain[173]. However, it is clear that each method is gradually becoming obsolete. In the United States, lethal injection is now the subject of genuine debate. Some states[174] now advocate the use of a single injection. What appeared to be a revolutionary step *towards* murder with dignity is, in the end, short-lived. The three products commonly injected in the majority of protocols[175], one of which is prohibited by veterinary practice in some states, are not without

---

173. Eight of the executing states have never disclosed the composition of the lethal injection cocktail they use.

174. Ohio and Washington in particular.

175. Sodium thiopental, an anaesthetic supposed to act within 10 seconds, pancuronium bromide to paralyze muscles, and potassium chloride to stop the heart.

their flaws[176]. Lethal injections sometimes turn out to be veritable butcheries, even justifying moratoria, as in California for example. Supposed to give death within seven minutes, injections have to be repeated because of incorrect dosage; injection with electric syringes has had to be abandoned because of malfunctions; catheter insertion sometimes takes up to 45 minutes, if the veins are difficult to find or prick, particularly when the death row inmate is a former intravenous drug user. Unless it is widely practised, as is the case in Texas at Huntsville prison, where almost one person a week is executed, lethal injection by non-medical prison staff is a bit like entrusting open-heart surgery to a plumber, however experienced.

The democratic need to tell without showing too much

The death penalty is undoubtedly less popular than it once was. It's a far cry from the spectacle of torment[177] of the recent era of public lynchings, and a sign of a notable evolution in the ability to channel violence. In this process, the spectacle of killing is reserved for those concerned: the executed person's relatives, the victims' relatives, prison

---

176. In 2010, governments ran out of sodium thiopental. The American laboratory Hospira, the world's only manufacturer of thiopental, decided to abandon production of this anaesthetic, notably under pressure from NGOs such as Reprieve, the World Coalition Against the Death Penalty and ECPM, but also under the injunction of the Italian government, which refused to allow a substance intended for executions to be produced on its territory. Ironically, "since the end of summer 2010, when several American states turned to Europe to make up for a national shortage of thiopental, six American death row inmates have filed a complaint in Washington against the Federal Drug Administration, which they accuse of having illegally authorized the import of thiopental, their lawyers announced on February 6. The complaint asks that the U.S. Food and Drug Administration (FDA) be found guilty of violating the law when it failed to prevent certain states from importing this anesthetic from Europe in the fall". "Abandonment of Thiopental production: a victory for ECPM and the Coalition", *Journal de l'abolition*, Paris, ECPM, December 2010. In addition, the Danish pharmaceutical company Lundbeck became the supplier of pentobarbital, which several states purchased to replace sodium thiopental. For more than six months, this laboratory dithered before taking the necessary steps to control the distribution of pentobarbital, so that it would be accessible only to the medical sector. See http://thepentobarbitalexperiment.wordpress.com

177. FOUCAULT (Michel), *Surveiller et punir*, Paris, Flammarion, 1975.

staff and journalists. And yet, in the United States, there is no reluctance to talk about the killing process, which is simply the expression of what the law authorizes. The retentionists know they are in the majority. It's not so much a desire to trivialize as a free demonstration of what cannot be hidden. While the United States suffers from a lack of debate on the death penalty, combined with almost total ignorance of the realities that govern this sentence, we have to acknowledge a fairly democratic transparency in the process used, with free access to the list of death row inmates executed or to be executed for each state, their names and criminal records, etc. The dates of execution are known to the public and the public at large. Execution dates are known to the general public, relayed timidly in the newspapers, and sometimes public press conferences are held following a killing to immediately communicate all the details.

In Utah, for example, when Ronnie Lee Gardner was executed on June 15, 2010, a major press conference was held at 2 a.m., attended by some twenty television, radio and print journalists, and foreign crews. Almost as if it were the launch of a commercial product, everyone received a press kit with colored dividers, and a CD-Rom featuring photos of the execution chamber and the chair on which the condemned man would be strapped before being shot. Because this was an exceptional killing by firing squad, in accordance with the condemned man's choice, the Utah prison administration chose to publicize it and accredit eight national and local journalists, who held a press conference in front of their own colleagues after the officials' speeches. In this way, everything seemed particularly transparent and limpid for anyone wishing to take an interest in this morbid situation. The details of the life ebbing away, the blood flowing, the last muscular reflexes - everything was recorded and expressed publicly, without shame or shame. But the secret of the show remained closely guarded. In 2010, it's still acceptable to "say", but perhaps less appropriate to "show". It's the beginning of an announced end to capital punishment, the beginning of a political and collective awakening, towards a softening of what a society can justify in the name of the good, and what it can assume on an institutional scale. And so it is that capital punishment has always disappeared, surreptitiously, through the back door, suppressing first its ostentatious dimension and then its own reality.

Control the details of death to minimize the risks

Penalties in the United States are geared to the ambition of absolute control, just as Michel Foucault[178] concluded about the historical evolution of the right to punish. It's almost like the development of an art of killing in which nothing is left to chance: the "techniques of death". To kill in the name of justice is to generate pain, resentment, embarrassment and even regret, all of which we, executors and jurors alike, have to live with. This problem of conscience is notably expressed in the decision of the French Medical Association to require its members not to take part in executions. Even if the medical profession is the most capable of skillfully inserting catheters into veins, dosing the product and reacting to any hazard that could jeopardize the protocol, it has been accepted from the outset that to treat is not to kill, even in the name of justice. Because[179] medical staff have officially refused to be associated with killing, to be accomplices in the morbid acts of justice, injections are carried out by prison staff, who are given a few hours' training to enable them to inject veins. In some cases, ex-Vietnam veterans are also recruited, as they are well-versed in the use of needles. Kevin Cooper, whom we met on death row in San

---

178. FOUCAULT (Michel), *op. cit.*

179. On this subject, see Death Penalty Information Center: "The American Medical Association (AMA) and the National Association of Emergency Medical Technicians (NAEMT) have issued statements reminding all their members of the ethical obligation not to participate in legal executions. AMA President William G. Plested III points out that the AMA prohibits all medical professionals from participating in executions, not least because it destroys public confidence in the medical profession. The NAEMT adds that complicity in executions is contrary to the ethical precepts and objectives of the medical profession." Nevertheless, in some states, notably California and Missouri, a doctor whose identity is kept secret takes part in executions.

Quentin, California, remembers the days leading up to his execution in 2004, which was finally suspended a few hours beforehand: "The administration took me aside to explain how they were going to inject the poisons. They checked the condition of my veins, because sometimes it's when the needles are inserted that things go wrong. At the same time, they were trying to reassure me. I think they wanted to be sure that I was going to be able to stand the wait before the date. One of his relatives, who comes in every week to meet him and support him, explains: "He suffered from trauma following this episode, and for weeks afterwards. He remained particularly excited and nervous. There's no psychological support on death row here in California. Credits are cut, so everyone fends for themselves."

In most countries, execution protocols are written down. Each phase is timed, and the execution rooms are organized accordingly, each inspired by the recommendations obtained empirically by each state. However, each state is free to organize its own killing operations, and there are no specifications at federal level. Recently, in Utah, the execution of Ronnie Lee Gardner by firing squad forced the authorities to establish a specific execution protocol. A stage was built, with a sort of screen forming the backdrop. A large wooden chair was fixed to it, equipped with a headrest and numerous leather straps to secure the body of the executioner to the chair, at numerous points of contact. Sandbags were placed on either side of the chair, on the platform, to cushion any shots that failed to hit their human target. The whole set was uniformly painted in a very dark grey, almost black, to absorb any ostentatious bloodshed. The five shooters were to fire from an adjoining room through a horizontal loophole. The execution, scheduled to take place in the killing room[180], was scheduled "from midnight". This is how the[181] press reported the event: "When a prison official opened the curtain to reveal the execution chamber to witnesses, the condemned

---

180. Last used for the lethal injection of Joseph Mitchell Parsons in 1999.

181. SANCHEZ (Ray), "Ronnie Lee Gardner executed by firing squad in Utah", *ABC Good Morning America*, June 18, 2010.

man, Ronnie Lee Gardner, was already strapped into the execution chair. His gaze swept the room at the Draper, Utah, prison, but he appeared calm, even appeased, witnesses said. This was in stark contrast to his life dotted with drugs, sexual abuse and general violence. When asked if he had anything to say, Gardner simply replied, 'No, I have nothing to say.' A black hood was pulled over his shaved head; a small target was attached to his heart. A barely audible countdown was interrupted by two successive loud 'booms'. It was fifteen minutes to midnight. After a quarter-century on death row, Gardner, aged 49, was the first man to be executed in Utah by firing squad in 14 years. 'He clenched his fists and then released them,' says radio host Doug Fabrizio, one of the small group of witnesses. 'And then he clenched his fist again.' A doctor took Gardner's pulse on both sides of his neck. When the black hood was removed to check Gardner's pupils with a beam of light, his earthy-skinned face was made visible for a brief moment. He was pronounced dead at midnight and seventeen minutes."

As with all executions in the USA, two rooms are specifically dedicated to the executioner. One for the authorities, accompanied by the victims' families; this connivance underlines the assumed purpose of a killing designed to satisfy them. The other is dedicated to the witnesses of the executed man. While some watch their loved ones being murdered, others hope to find relief in the spectacle of the murder of the perpetrator of a crime that has affected them personally. This is how justice is served in 34 US states in 2011.

According to the former warden of Walls Prison in Huntsville, who oversaw 89 executions, last wishes were often "pardons" and messages to the families. He points out that, in the old days, the sentence was accepted, with no desire to rebel. There was undoubtedly a feeling of submission to a severe and implacable sentence, against which there was no point in contesting. These were the times of fatalism, identified in all societies, in the face of inescapable events that it would have been foolish to fight. It was this same fatalism that was imposed by the all-too-frequent death resulting from war, childbirth and infection. A death accepted as we digest the bends in an inescapable destiny, with only relative resistance. In this age of desired immortality and the fantasy of eternal youth in a society in search of continual asepsis, it's likely that death will no longer be surrounded by the same fatalism.

The most common last meal is a hamburger with *French fries*. The budget for this national delicacy varies from prison to prison. Ms. L., a criminology student at the University of San Francisco, wonders: "What sense does it make to want to satisfy the taste buds of someone you're going to kill, i.e. from whom you're going to take the principal?" Between $25 and $40, that's how much the administration is willing to allocate for this ultimate pleasure that knotted appetites don't always allow to be consumed. Jim Willett, former warden of Walls prison in Huntsville, Texas, recalls: "I organized 89 executions. Some of them eat a lot, and I've always been surprised by that," he adds: "Smoking has been banned since 1996, but I always supplied them with cigarettes if they wanted them until 1998. Some of them smoked almost a pack in their afternoon."

The perverse effects of giving death

In an instant, the execution puts an end to existences, as if it were a matter of eliminating intrinsically dangerous individuals whose pathogenic behaviors were to be repeated ad infinitum. This is what citizens imagine when they argue the usefulness of this irreversible sentence. It's the expression of an irrational fear that tends to picture the representations given by media, literary and film narratives, very much in vogue in the United States, suggesting that a serial killer lurks behind every criminal. Here again, between the passions that rule and the absence of knowledge to fuel a reasoning process, opinions wander and constitute the dregs of security policies and paranoid behavior. If you look closely, most crimes are the satisfaction of unprecedented moments of honor or intoxication, which are what they were only when circumstances coincide in a way that no probability can predict again. It is these moments of drifting that justice punishes with this long confinement with a fatal outcome. As long as society at large does not take a moderate view of recidivism, and as long as citizens do not fight this propensity to cry wolf even before the danger appears, criminal sentences in general, and the death sentence in particular, will remain the irrational breeding ground for the worst indignities. Very often, conviction and incarceration are more than enough to raise awareness and prevent the repetition of murderous acts. However, the death penalty, like life without parole, by removing any prospect of life, leads the majority of convicts to scuttle their own image as individuals with nothing left to lose. This leads to violent behavior, even in prison, which, in the eyes of the administration, justifies draconian security measures. If you're going to be killed like an animal, why not kill again? We must understand that it is the death penalty itself that takes on this dimension of "nothing left to lose", transforming men into a mass of unrestrained hatred and violence. It is also the exemplary indignities of the judicial system as a whole that spurs revolt and disobedience. What remains human in death row, other than the prospects of a better life that some nourish in the meagre hopes raised by the incessant shuttling between appeal courts, state or federal supreme courts, or the factual or imaginary certainty of one day being freed as an innocent man?

At the same time, the execution makes the victims relive their grief and plunges them into an internal conflict between, on the one hand, the resurgence of a vengeful hatred legitimized by the paroxysm of emotions felt when the initial crime was committed, and on the other, the awareness of being caught up in a legal procedure at the hands of the prison administration, a dangerous and delicate game in which they become unwilling accomplices. And yet, it is from this legal murder that the victims' families expect comfort. In reality, so many months and years pass between the initial sentence and the execution, an infinite time during which some live at liberty at a distance from others in prison, that in the end the execution appears to be the final point in a story that everyone could have mourned if it hadn't been for the fact that they had to wait for the verdict of death to be carried out. When the emotion caused by the crime has subsided, some victims explain that they would have been content with a life sentence had the law not offered them the death penalty. In other words, even though capital punishment is often called for, it could easily be abolished. Two days after the execution of her husband's murderer, Veldean Kirk confided: "I wanted the prosecutor to ask for the death penalty, because it's part of the law, and I thought it was fairer in this case. Ronnie Lee Gardner had killed many times, even in prison. But if the law had only provided for life, I wouldn't have minded."

Everyone considers themselves subject to the law, whether it advocates prison or death row. The law imposes itself symbolically without being contradicted; it's an endorsed norm, the respect of which is certainly to the credit of American history, the history of a recent country, homogenized by a Constitution that some consider to be inspired by the Bible or God himself. In the end, since only a very small proportion of the population of the United States is involved, and provided that political pressure and the sometimes perverse influence of the media are overcome, the political courage required for abolition should not represent a major risk. This is borne out by a May 2006 poll by the Gallup Institute, which shows that support for the death penalty averages 65% (down from 80% in 1994), but that if respondents were given the choice of a life sentence without parole, more would choose the latter (48%) than the death penalty (47%)[182].

For others, the execution represents an event in which it's important to take part; whether it's the eight journalists invited to Ronnie Lee Gardner's firing squad in Utah, who experienced the moment as a local and even national event; or the little girl who came to watch her grandfather's killer being put to death, and who confesses to having

---

182. Results of Gallup poll conducted in May 2006.

no other motivation than the idea of witnessing in real life a scene of gore that she hopes will live up to cinematic virtuality. Jamie, 28, says: "This is a once-in-a-lifetime opportunity. To see someone shot dead live! […] It was much cleaner than I imagined. I thought there would be blood spurting everywhere, like in the movies. In the end, it was quick, almost frustrating. But I'm glad I was there." Whether it's the five shooters who make up the platoon, chosen from among 200 other candidates, less fortunate volunteers, the execution, unless it has become a morbid routine, as is the case in Texas, is an event in which some take astonishing pride. For some, there is honor in killing. It's a double-edged honor, which, when closely observed, also leaves a divided, fragmented and bitter emotion. Despite the certainty of having performed a legal act justified by society, of having witnessed it, of having been its active or passive accomplice, death is not always easy to apprehend. Between embarrassment and indifference, the journalists accredited to witness the execution had varying assessments: "It was quick, clean, almost clinical […] it wasn't like in the movies […] all we heard was a big 'bang', then nothing […] after the shots, he kept moving his left arm a little, so we finally wondered if he was dead […] it wasn't violent, contrary to what you might think." One of the eight journalists was the only one to observe, "I grew up with a Winchester and I've been used to shooting with it since I was a kid, and despite that, I think it was violent, because it was the death of a man."

In our contemporary history, this is neither an everyday nor a trivial moment. Whether we like it or not, there's something irrational and disproportionate about taking a life. And we all have to admit to a disturbing but undoubtedly very real idea: that some people are less easy to kill than others. This politically incorrect observation applies to victims of murder as much as to victims of capital punishment. Because beyond the universality of the human being and the rights that go with it, there is the singularity of the individual, on which mourning and acceptance will depend, on which the legitimization of the act will more or less adhere, deep down, in a personal and silent way.

Chapter 10:
Future Prospects

In contrast to other countries, where the death penalty is a very openly arbitrary penal object, used sometimes sparingly, sometimes excessively, but without the arguments that justify it ever being updated in favor of its self-evident retention, in the United States, the death penalty is an elaborate mechanism, written down, protocolized, instrumentalized according to the times, thus summoning up many aspects of American society, its trajectory and the system that governs it. Herein lies the curiosity of the researcher, the passion of the activists, and the optimism of the urgent need to abolish the death penalty. Paradoxically, the death penalty in the United States is rooted in a culture of retribution, of fear to appease, of severity that pays, of indulgence that weakens, and of the certainty that vengeance is necessary to deter. Yet the edifice cracks regularly, and things can change rapidly in this young society that always knows how to bounce back. The length of time that has elapsed since the reintroduction of the death penalty in 1976, between sentencing and execution, is an expression of the jolts of abolition that hide their true face. For, discreetly, these delays empty the death penalty of its true meaning. Detached from the crime committed, the sentence becomes an obsolete penal object, the words emptied and will only embody a symbolic punishment, which although still murderous and unjust, takes with it the little rational basis that can still support it in a democratic society.

The cracks in an archaic penal system

In the context of open discrimination, less than 50 years ago, public lynchings were still tolerated. The spectacle of the humiliating killing of African-Americans, guilty or not, independently of any legal proceedings, was still familiar in some regions. Since then, the death penalty has become merely institutionalized, and the processes involved in putting people to death are constantly called into question in the supposedly virtuous quest for a clean and humane execution, as an act of justice that too much ostentatious suffering would decidedly dishonor. The ineptitude of capital punishment reveals its face day after day. The myth of its deterrent effect is running out of steam[183]. The mass execution of the thousands of condemned men languishing on American death rows would resemble a mass slaughter likely to be requalified by many. The millions of dollars that a death sentence costs under the current conditions of trial and appeal are difficult to reconcile with state ruin. Publicity about the discriminatory nature of the death penalty reaches a wider audience. The execution of proven innocents[184] renders justice immoral while underlining its fallibility. The population is becoming increasingly educated, giving everyone critical arguments. In this shifting landscape, the death penalty is gradually beginning to be seen as an institution that can be amended. It is a sentence so gangrenous that even some of its defenders seem aware of its programmed finitude. The boat is taking on water on all sides, which is rekindling the fervor of activist retentionists, ready to make any compromise, moral or intellectual, to maintain the legitimacy of murder in the collective consciousness, as long as it is cloaked in the morbid trappings of justice. Bettye Wilkinson, retired curator of the Texas Department of Corrections, now volunteers at the Huntsville Prison Museum, confides in a speech mixing contradictions and certainties: "I've always defended the death penalty, but today I'd be

---

183. In a study by the Death Penalty Information Center, only 5% of criminologists agree that the death penalty has a deterrent effect, compared with 88% who disagree.

184. Even if none of these "executions of innocents" is officially recognized in the contemporary history of the death penalty in the United States.

happy with life without parole. It's not that I've become against it, but I think the death penalty will eventually be abolished, which may take several years. I realize that since there's been 'real' life, there's been less death penalty. That's why I think it's no longer necessary, and can be abolished… I'm waiting for the legislators to do it. I don't know when it's going to happen, but it will happen, even here in Texas."

From a legal point of view, the fight has also reached an advanced stage: in Mississippi, 15 death row inmates have filed a complaint claiming that *the death penalty is unconstitutional*. Despite this, a Salt Lake City law student[185] confides: "Out of a class of over 30 people in law classes, only 2 students were against the death penalty." It's a safe bet that in a majority of states in the USA, as in many countries, the death penalty will disappear surreptitiously through a back door. Progress is being made here and there, leading to a gradual scarcity of sentences and executions[186]. From this can be deduced the abolition of facts that can prepare the electorate for a political decision. This process is slow, because it works in stages, but it operates in a country where everything can suddenly speed up.

---

185. Salt Lake City, the capital of Utah, is 50% Mormon and belongs to the Church of the Latter Day Saints. They are not opposed to the death penalty on principle. They have no official discourse or position.

186. "According to Death Penalty Information Center forecasts, the number of death sentences in 2010 is 114, close to the previous year's historically low level and about 64% lower than in 1996, when death sentences reached a record 315. California leads the country with 29 death sentences, about the same number as the previous year. Many retentionist states such as Virginia, Georgia, Missouri and Indiana did not issue a single death sentence in 2010. […] On December 2, 2010, the Bureau of Justice Statistics (BJS) […] came to the same conclusion, namely that the number of death sentences handed down in 2009 represented the lowest since 1973. According to the BJS, 112 people were sentenced to death in 2009, compared with 119 in 2008. […] The BJS also reports that the time from conviction to execution for those executed in 2009 was 14 years, the longest recorded since the return of the death penalty." "While the use of the death penalty continues to decline, the majority of Americans who support it are declining, the number of executions has fallen by 12%: death sentences are at an all-time low", in *The Death Penalty in 2010. Year-end report*, Death Penalty Information Center, December 2010.

Even in Texas, opinions are increasingly critical. Paradoxically, since 2001, the state has even decided to increase funding for the public defender system. This gradual trend is perceived by a majority of abolitionists. This is the joint opinion of journalists, criminology professors and activists. Steve Hall, director of the StandDown Texas Project, explains: "In 2001, they created the Texas Fair Defense Act, under which the state gives money to the indigent. What we saw then was an increase in *public defender offices*. It's a huge change, we've got lawyers who do just that now, they specialize in death penalty cases, in representing appeals. And there's also a special office for appeals. Many states have set up these offices." This decision is seen as the sign of a slow, gradual evolution, the outcome of which nobody knows, in favor of a reduction in the number of cases where the death penalty is applied. In principle, capital punishment is not called into question. However, among moderates and non-militants, whether Republican or Democrat, there are often expressions of a desire to see its use restricted. Ideally, it should be reserved for guilty parties who are certain to be guilty. It should not be applied to those who credibly attest that they have changed their personality sufficiently to no longer represent a danger[187]. Lastly, it should only be applied to the most terrible crimes, most often involving children, or any form of configuration showing the implacable relief between the dangerousness of the perpetrator on the one hand and the fragility of the victim on the other.

What's more, it's becoming quite common for militant retentionists to refuse to speak out or debate. As if their arguments today were no longer so audible, credible or legitimate. As if it would become politically incorrect to take responsibility tomorrow for having defended the death penalty yesterday. Kent Scheidegger, a jurist with a pro-death penalty victims' rights organization in Sacramento, was difficult to persuade. He refused to take part in the research because he feared

---

187. This indulgence will probably never apply to those on death row who, by their case and their person, stigmatize an indelible evil, i.e. serial killers, paedophiles and other sex criminals.

his arguments would be ridiculed. According to lawyers representing death row inmates, Debra Saunders, a pro-death penalty journalist with the *San Francisco Chronicle,* writes regularly without ever being interested in the arguments they develop in their defense[188]. In her own words: "The problem with abolitionists is that they're so against the death penalty that they never look at the crime committed!" Although she admits that she doesn't share her retentionist convictions with everyone around her, she finds that it's becoming impossible to stand up to abolitionist activists. The balance of power has shifted in favor of abolition among *those in the know,* some of whom are therefore the decision-makers. Just as a ball changes sides, today it is increasingly legitimate to allow abolitionist arguments to penetrate public discourse.

Social death rather than physical death: the choice of perpetuity[189]

Bettye Wilkinson, a saleswoman at the Huntsville Prison Museum, confides, "Now we realize it's time to stop killing. Life without parole is enough even for the most serious crimes." This frequent comment attests to the fact that, despite all the eminently questionable aspects of life imprisonment with no possibility of release, the long non-existence of this sentence in the panoply of criminal sanctions justified in some people's minds the existence and use of the death penalty, designed to protect society forever from the presumed dangers of an individual denied the ability to change. With this new sentence, which Texas was the last state to adopt in 2005, combined with the tightening

---

188. The California attorneys for Mumia Abu-Jamal, incarcerated in Pittsburgh, and Kevin Cooper, incarcerated in San Quentin, San Francisco, are up in arms about the incriminating papers against their respective clients by Ms. Saunders, who allegedly never bothered to investigate the "cases" or interview them as any journalist would.

189. "*Life without parole*" means life without parole. No circumstances can justify release. This sentence also constitutes torture, removing freedom and keeping a human being locked in a cell with no other prospect. Physiological life may be preserved, but social death is confirmed, and this provision, whose unrestricted authority brooks no indulgence or exception, reduces humanity to a subservient relationship.

of prison seals - in other words, since the new establishments have become impregnable fortresses from which escapes are now virtually impossible - public opinion is now guaranteed never to come across the perpetrators of the worst crimes on the street again. Collective fears are beginning to be assuaged by permanent confinement.

As in many retentionist countries, in the United States, if you kill a police officer, you run the risk of being sentenced to death. There is a sacralization of the forces of law and order that locks in any criticism and discourages any revolt. Robert R. Bryan, a criminal lawyer in San Francisco, explains: "The authority of the police also comes from this, they easily become untouchables as a result, like organs of a second society in which there would be citizens and supermen whose lives would have a higher price." It's a comparable phenomenon that inspires the veneration of firefighters and other firefighters, or that nurtured around soldiers sent to defend U.S. values in Iraq or Afghanistan. Patricia Lykos, District Attorney of Harris County, Texas, justifies it in these terms: "The value of life is more important when a police officer is killed, because it is society that is attacked. No civilized society can tolerate waiting for the life of someone who saves the lives of others." Yet recently in Texas, the murderer of a police officer escaped the death penalty. In an unprecedented move, life imprisonment was preferred to execution[190]. This event is one of the signs of a gradual shift away from the death sentence towards life imprisonment, the application of which can, however, in many cases, also prove abusive. Faith in the law and in the institutions of justice leads to a general endorsement. The day the death penalty is no longer legal, the day this sentence disappears from the penal system, then, despite nostalgic reactionaries, the American people will be satisfied with the application of the law when it only advocates life imprisonment. In fact, since the introduction of

---

190. In Texas, two police killers were sentenced to 60 years in prison on Monday June 7, 2010. Andres Nava-Maldonado and Xiomara Mendez-Rosales were found guilty of murder and criminal activity for the shooting death of Houston police officer Henry Canales.

"*life without parole*", the number of death sentences in Texas has fallen, particularly in the all-too-famous Harris County[191].

On several occasions, it was also mentioned, albeit timidly, that some retentionists fear the tide is turning. As the slow march towards abolition accelerates, some will find it difficult to identify with being perceived as a murderer or a barbarian. Some men also refuse to take on the role of executioner for fear of one day being prosecuted for killing. A young man I met in Huntsville commented on the situation of executioners: "The people who carry out executions here kill over 30 people a year, and they're never bothered. But one day that's going to change and some of them know it, it's starting to scare them." It's a latent awareness, which is certainly part of a series of signals pointing here and there, little by little, to cracks in the cultural edifice on which capital punishment is based in the United States. And because it's often reassuring to put things into perspective, Americans remember the struggles it took to abolish slavery, and to achieve the civil rights movement from the Civil War to Martin Luther King and his descendants. It's a long and tedious struggle, as we all know. It is also unfairly organized. However, abolitionists are convinced of one thing: to advance the process of civilization while respecting human dignity. Rick Halperin sums it up this way: "I know that the death penalty will be abolished in this country; the process has already begun. We're not talking about *if*, but *when*. I think it's going to be a long struggle, a lot more people are going to be killed before it stops, but we're going to reach a point where we're going to have to look at our past. Here we are in 2010, we're looking at this America, which practiced slavery, and we're stunned. How could this country maintain slavery for 246 years and think it was right? That's what everyone thought. In those days, it was the norm, just as the death penalty is for us. But societies evolve, and they do so at a pace that is as slow as it is frustrating. That's

---

191. This is the county of the city of Houston, famous for being the biggest purveyor of death row inmates in Texas.

Chapter 10: Future Prospects

what's going to happen in this country with the death penalty. Sooner or later, we will reach a stage where this people, as a whole, will accept the idea that killing people in the name of the law is wrong. That it does our country no good. But we're still a long way from that day."

This optimism is also expressed by David Atwood, founder of the Texas Coalition, when he says: "Our goal is to get more and more citizens against the death penalty, to educate them. When we have enough of them, politicians will take up the issue. It's a citizens' movement that's going to change things. The civil rights movement in the '60s was ultimately quite similar. It also came mainly from the South. Before that, the abolition of slavery was also *citizens against slavery*. It's a tough fight. Abolishing the death penalty is another step towards civilization, towards humanity. And I think we'll get there." In the meantime, Robert R. Bryan explains that "the death penalty is a political need [...] Which indicates how much our society is failing. Such violence is very unfavorable for young people, the state is setting a bad example. We must be able to do better, to have faith in human beings, to be more ambitious for our country, to wish for better justice".

CHAPTER 11:
ABOLITION STRATEGIES

The argument of the cost of the death penalty

Politicians seem fallible whenever they express indulgence. On the contrary, they need to appear strong, to symbolize power, and thus promote an ever more punitive system. Hence the need to find abolitionist arguments that are far removed from any ideology, in this case embodied in a critical reflection on the cost of the death penalty. More and more newspaper articles are denouncing the cost of capital punishment in the United States. In fact, because of the incessant back-and-forth between the various levels of state courts and their counterparts in the federal courts, and because of the investigations and expert reports required to support the prosecution or the defense, the cost of the death penalty has become exorbitant in some states. The death penalty in California costs taxpayers $114 million a year, more than the cost of life imprisonment. They have paid more than $250 million for each of the state's executions[192]. In Texas, the average death row case costs $2.3 million, roughly three times the cost of incarcerating a single individual in a maximum-security prison cell for

---

192. TEMPEST (Rone), "Death row often means a long life", *Los Angeles Times*, March 6, 2005.

40 years[193]. Norman Hile analyzes the situation thus: "California is bankrupt, and we'd save millions of dollars without the death penalty. It's an easy argument, but it doesn't work either. We've made savings everywhere, on education, on roads, yet they don't want to save on the death penalty. Personally, I'd rather see the money go to schools or the healthcare system." Prof. Shatz, from the University of San Francisco, adds: "Since 1976, California has spent between $3 and $5 billion more than it would have if there had been no death penalty, for just 13 executions in 32 years, while we have no money left to improve law and order, among other things." On this argument, Ohio, Montana and Maryland have recently made several attempts to draw up abolition projects, the main aim being to clean up precariously balanced public accounts. Colorado and Connecticut are probably just as close to abolition. To date, however, these initiatives have been failures, even if they do testify to a political will associated with the emergence of a public debate[194], admittedly fuelled more by financial than ideological motivations, but nonetheless a source of hope for the months and years to come[195].

---

193. HOPPE (Christy), "Executions cost Texas millions", *Dallas Morning News*, March 8, 1992.

194. "The costs of maintaining capital punishment are enormous. In this time of tight budgets and budget cuts, Illinois has wisely decided to redirect tax dollars to support victims' families. [...] Maryland, like Illinois, has studied its capital punishment system thoroughly. We know that the system will never be free of human error, that it is racist and unevenly applied in our state. It doesn't even deter murder, but costs us about three times as much as incarcerating murderers for life. If the General Assembly refuses to debate and vote to abolish the death penalty in 2011, another year of losses awaits us. At least six death penalty cases are pending in Maryland. They will drain resources we desperately need to prevent crimes, maintain safe prisons, and assist victims. The time to end them is simply now." GIBSON (Stephanie), associate professor at the University of Baltimore, "The time to abolish the death penalty is now," *Baltimore Sun*, March 20, 2011.

195. GRAVELAND (Bill), "For the second time in four years, proposed legislation to abolish and substitute a sentence of life without parole was presented to the Montana Senate Judiciary Committee, which voted in favor," *The Canadian Press*, March 19, 2011.

Meanwhile, the death penalty in most states resembles a self-imposed life sentence. It has become nothing more than a symbolic punishment, a totem brandished by politicians, which legislators are finding hard to change, for two reasons. On the one hand, the very high crime rate does not provide a favorable context, and on the other, political courage is lacking both at the executive level and in the judiciary, since state judges are elected on the same campaign criteria: to be *"tough on crime"* in all circumstances. David Atwood finally acknowledges that one of the obstacles to abolition in his country is that there is "no national leader to carry the abolitionist project forward. Not even Barack Obama. He adds: "All the politicians fear for their careers if they speak out."

Western democracies no longer have this problem, as abolition has been achieved and legally locked in at all levels of the hierarchy of legal norms: national and supranational. In the United States, utilitarian arguments need to be developed, such as those that have worked in New Mexico and are now being developed, particularly in California, with regard to cost, in line with the American maxim *"Money* Talks"[196].

The criticism of this approach, assuming it is exclusive, is that it omits the foundation of abolition embodied in the prohibition on denying the right to life. In practice, however, and to absolve themselves of any angelism, American abolitionists have to play into the hands of their own opponents, in this case developing a pragmatic vision, devoid of ideology and morality, based on the economic question. This point of view is criticized by those who fear that the politicians are putting in place a streamlined penal system that would eventually allow the death sentence and execution to be carried out without the hindrance of numerous appeals, as some states are currently studying. Given the political excesses of the past and probably of the future, this concern is no doubt not entirely unfounded, and makes this short-term argu-

---

196. "Money is king".

Chapter 11: Abolition Strategies

ment in times of crisis a risky angle that requires us to bear in mind an essential question: can abolition do without political courage?

From a strategic point of view, the basis of the economic argument for abolition suffers from another intrinsic criticism. For by basing abolition solely on circumstantial arguments, fluctuating with the times, abolition can have no solid foundation, especially in a society in perpetual renewal. As long as the idea is not translated into a non-derogable principle, abolition will remain precarious and potentially unstable, as it is intimately linked to a conjunction of events. What justifies abolition one day may justify the opposite the next. As Rick Halperin puts it: "I'm in favor of abolition on moral rather than economic grounds, and of a culture of abolition. Because one day the economy will be better, and we'll be able to say, 'We've got money, let's start killing again!' Without sweeping aside this economic argument, which speaks to the greatest number of people, there remains, as a second act, the need to achieve an irreversible cultural, legal and political lock.

With this in mind, and given the retentionist forces at work, many American abolitionists are promoting a fight without limits and without distinction of weapons, with the aim of uniting all those who, for one reason or another, would be in a position to move the current lines. At the extreme, it can even involve an association, which a priori would be considered unnatural, with the forces of law and order, who hold a very important symbolic representation at the heart of American society. According to a recent study organized by the Death Penalty Information Center in 2009[197], police officers, again for practical reasons as opposed to any ideological or moral point of view, are increasingly opposed to capital punishment, which they deem useless and dangerous. 57% of them believe that the death penalty

---

197. Smart on Crime: reconsidering the death penalty in tough economic times, the National Police Chiefs Survey, puts capital punishment at the bottom of law enforcement priorities, Death Penalty Information Center, 2009.

has no deterrent effect[198], and only 2% attribute public disorder to too moderate a use of it[199]. And because the police, whose aura is skilfully nurtured by central government, understand only their own language, their complicity in the abolition process requires that they be allowed to appropriate a vision of public order without the death penalty. It is therefore urgent to present abolitionist arguments to them as soon as they are trained, before they are completely reframed by the day-to-day reality of their professional lives.

Involving victims more effectively

Victims express their feelings about convicts without knowing what they go through on a daily basis. For them, the murderer is just a name associated with a sentence. *Deserved* suffering materializes behind the word *prison* in abolitionist countries, and behind the expression *death penalty* in retentionist countries. In one case, we await release, in the other execution. These are two opposing worlds that would benefit from coming together. Just as restorative justice was practiced in some African countries before colonization, American society would also benefit from bringing guilty parties and victims' families together. For the former, this would establish a possible narrative beyond the judicial discourse, and for the latter, it would enable them to exist beyond the crime they have committed. Several states have already set up mediation programs between inmates and victims or victims' families. In Texas, this measure is even enshrined in the Code of Criminal

---

198. The deterrent effect is also denied by other corporations in the USA. According to a survey of past and present presidents of the country's leading criminological societies, 88% of experts reject the notion that the death penalty is a deterrent (RADELET and LACOCK, "Do executions lower homicide rates?: The views of leading criminologists", *The Journal of Criminal Law & Criminology*, vol. XCIX, no. 2, Northwestern University, School of Law, Chicago, 2009).

199. According to the survey, the factors disrupting law and order are: lack of financial resources (20%), use of psychotropic drugs (20%), family problems (14%), lack of programs for the mentally ill (12%), overcrowded courts (7%), ineffective prosecution (6%), widespread gun ownership (5%), gangs (3%), insufficient use of the death penalty (2%).

Procedure. At the same time, even today, victims' families are refused by the prison administration when they wish to make contact with the criminal. Yet, more than anywhere else, and because the death penalty appears to be a necessity in the arsenal of vengeful justice, encouraging forms of contact between the families of victims and perpetrators appears to be a pacifying device to defuse the desire to kill and any other form of compensatory violence. This is what a young woman who came to attend the execution of Michael Perry, the young murderer of her mother and brother, testifies, vainly confronting her own pain with that of the executed man's mother: "Actually, I feel sorry for Michael's mother. I imagine it must be very hard to see her son executed this afternoon, tied with his arms crossed on the injection table. Just like Jesus. But she never tried to contact me either. Can she imagine what we've been through all these years? This grief caused by her son's actions?"

Rather than having a penal policy that pits the good guys, who have suffered, against the bad guys, who have caused suffering, according to a locked Manichaeism, it would indeed be ambitious to think of a means of reconciling these two entities, each respectively prey to real and legitimate pain. Given the Christianization of the population in the United States, monotheistic religions could be one of the vectors of this *reconciliation*, like the precepts of the New Testament, the forgiveness of Jesus, but also the highly symbolic rapprochement between Pope John Paul II and the man who tried to assassinate him, Mehmet Ali Agca. The sterility of Manichean opposition, both in its inability to appease consciences and feelings, to establish a bulwark against recidivism, and in its perversity in maintaining a hateful opposition at the heart of society, is certainly more costly socially than a genuine attitude of reparation and reconciliation. When we associate the pain of the condemned offender and his family with the crime committed, and the pain of the victims' families with the crime committed, we realize the extent to which the death penalty is a non-answer, a non-solution, a strange object that we don't know whether it responds to the institutionalized vengeance of a form of violence that the law has taken upon itself to channel, or to the fantasy of an effective, redemptive punishment to which we attribute dissuasive virtues.

In this sense, because the United States regularly promotes itself as a nation of pioneers, civil society should encourage this rapprochement and promote the idea. After executions, it is striking to note the correlation between the absence of remorse on the part of the condemned and the need for death on the part of victims' families. And yet, as the discussions progressed, it became clear that both sides would have benefited from a gradual rapprochement, in which the indispensable words of remorse and contrition must be asked, expressed and heard. The widow of a police officer who died as a result of an assault with a deadly weapon by a criminal in Utah explained a few days after the execution: "I forgave him a long time ago, and I think everyone in the family has done the same, except maybe one of my daughters. [...] But I think he owed me an apology. He could have written to me, or asked to speak to me by phone. But I would have liked to meet him, to talk to him face to face, not over the phone, but eye to eye. The prison management never gave me permission, and he didn't ask for it. It's a shame, I'm sorry for him and his family, but I feel at peace with it. It's over now." After the years between the crime committed and the execution, these expressions of remorse are ultimately more eagerly awaited than the death itself. What emerges from these speeches is a need to meet, an expression of hatred, but also a hidden desire to draw closer together, to silence the misunderstandings that put distance between people who are sometimes so close. This is the price of appeasing individual and collective passions in society. It's the road to civilization. Another woman confides her paradoxical emotions on leaving the execution of the murderer of her brother and mother: "I wanted to be there for my family, and I also wanted to hear words of forgiveness, an apology for what he did 15 years ago. [...] At the same time, I found it strange that someone so young would be killed." She adds: "It wasn't what I expected. In my nightmares, this guy was a monster. In fact, he was just a kid, crying for his mother. It scared me when I heard him speak just before the first injection. I used to think he should have been sentenced to life without the death penalty. But today, the fact that he doesn't apologize to the victims, to us, has turned him into a monster for good. As a result, I tell myself he got what he deserved."

On the one hand, the pain of the victims must be expressed to the perpetrator. On the other, the condemned person's medical history can help to ensure that the human dimension of the person whose death is desired is never overlooked. Last but not least, time acts, no matter what we say. Enemy or friend, time softens emotions, changes perceptions and temperaments. Death row inmates define themselves as different after years on death row. The person executed is often no longer the same individual as the one condemned.

If organized by associations and supported by the law and institutions, this rapprochement would be salutary in more ways than one. It would offer the comfort of reducing regrets on both sides. It would give meaning to intrinsically imperfect lives. It would steer society towards a response to violent instincts, rendering obsolete political rhetoric advocating callous severity. In every case, this ambition is a benefit and an asset. And beyond the pragmatic involvement of religions and all forms of education and culture in this mechanism, it is society as a whole, secular or religious, that should promote this philosophy, which saves lives, mental suffering and social violence.

Independently of the search for justice based on reconciling opposing issues, several American associations[200] promote abolition by highlighting the victims' point of view. Their soothing discourse, which is commonly assumed to be vengefully motivated, seems highly effective

---

200. Examples include: "Murder victims Family for reconciliation" (www.mvfr.org), "Journey of hope... From violence to healing" (www.journeyofhope.org) or "Murder victims family for human rights" (www.mvfhr.org).

insofar as it contradicts what the death penalty is so strongly defended for across the Atlantic: victim satisfaction. These activists, often tied up in the grief of losing a loved one to murder, demonstrate their conviction that the death penalty is in no way a desirable response to their grief. Their argument is all the more legitimate in that it destroys the arguments of pro-death penalty campaigners, who regularly trade on the pathos of the real victims of crime, to argue for a sentence that is globally perceived as an inescapable penal remedy. Victims' voices are increasingly effective in lobbying campaigns in favor of abolition. This lays the foundations for a reflection on forgiveness, respect for life and acceptance of the loss of a loved one, which can never be compensated for by the execution of another. This angle of view also reveals the extent to which the death penalty is a relentless machine, tirelessly creating new victims, in this case among the loved ones of the person the state is about to execute. As Brandie Gardner testifies on the day of her father's execution: "Tonight, the real victims are us!" Thanks to this view, it suddenly seems absurd to punish crime with crime, as summed up by the abolitionists' slogan: "Why do we kill people to show that killing is wrong?"[201]

201. "Why do we kill people to show that killing is wrong?"

CHAPTER 12:
THE MEANING OF A STRUGGLE

Examining the mechanisms that keep the death penalty alive in American democracy undeniably leads to the identification of situations that reason unravels, admitting that sometimes, depending on the circumstances, individuals can only be viewed through the prism of Manichaeism. Tammy Kirk, in the aftermath of the execution of her father's killer, describes how she sees things: "I feel sorry for Ronnie Lee Gardner's daughter. It must be hard to lose your father. But we have nothing to do with that family. They're all criminals. Well, almost… I mean, compared to us, they're nothing to do." Certainly, evil can be on the side of criminals whose past ignominy remains unregretted. More often than not, these people carry with them a chaotic history made up of emotional gaps and irreversible traumas, a whole set of factors which, if they don't excuse, at least explain and sometimes arouse a feeling of pity or compassion.

More aggressively, evil appears more embodied in the corrupt attitudes of those individuals, often privileged, who have the power to judge, condemn and execute, and who use these prerogatives in defiance of the law, circumstances and the popular conscience, to ultimately instrumentalize executions for personal ends. These are the unethical players in the police, judicial and political systems, who gain notoriety, money and power by putting their fellow human beings to death under false and indefensible pretences. Steve Hall, director of the StandDown Texas Project[202], explains: "Judges or District Attorneys are elected on the principle of severity. As a result, many District Attorneys refuse to allow DNA testing to be carried out, so as not to suggest that the system could be faulty and therefore dangerous for innocent people. Others accept, as is the case in Dallas County, where a Conviction Integrity Office has been set up to track down cases of innocence. So there are incredible disparities that no one talks about. [...] I also remember this prosecutor who had an affair with the District Attorney. The two of them arranged the prosecution and conviction. We didn't find out until last year, but the executions had already taken place. [...] It's really just justice disguised."

The social positions of these elected representatives make the accusation/defense relationship as inequitable as it is inextricable, daily abusing the ignorance of a population whose naivety is often knowingly maintained. Their official actions feed on the baser instincts of the human species, generating fear and paranoia, while their unofficial actions are advantageously masked by the power of influence and intimidation at their disposal. If they were exceptions, their mention in this text would be outrageous. But it must be admitted that corruption reigns in the United States, in many guises, among police officers and elected officials, both political and judicial, and every time it is exercised, it attests to and confirms what cannot be forgotten: the power to punish, and even more so the death penalty, is first and foremost a political weapon. The idea of justice is more often than not no more than a make-up for "dirty deeds", a wordless language that speaks to the masses of the poorest and least educated. This grand illusion develops in the context of a violent society, made up of precariousness and fear of tomorrow. A society that forgives little, in which

---

202. StandDown Texas Project: identification and advocacy of "best practices" in criminal justice, analysis of the specific Texas context, highlighting reform initiatives and emerging issues.

everything is a matter of individual combat and struggle, outlawing anything remotely resembling the idea of collective and state solidarity.

Of course, death row isn't just full of innocent people. Some of them have even committed horrible crimes. Angelism does not serve the cause of abolition. On closer inspection, however, it's likely that the perpetrators of American society's worst ills aren't the ones found on death row. With luck, sufficient financial means and the right connections, the privileged have the means to escape capital punishment. This is something the public can no longer ignore since the high-profile case of O.J. Simpson, who was finally exonerated after being accused of a double murder that would ordinarily have landed a poor anonymous man on the lethal injection table. And therein lies the paradoxically iniquitous dimension of American justice. It's a morbid injustice when it comes to the right to life. And it's hard to see how society can remedy these forms of iniquity. This realization alone should contribute to considering abolition as a relief. According to this scheme, unless you belong to the most influential and wealthiest 20% of American society, to be in favor of the death penalty is to act against your own best interests. In the United States, as elsewhere, only the poor, the ignorant and the voiceless are executed. It is also true, as Alexis de Tocqueville says[203], that the United States is undoubtedly more attached to liberty than to equality.

Until very recently, the rule in the United States was that the death certificate should be marked "homicide" or "legal homicide". This irony is reminiscent of the very essence of execution. Some retentionists also suffer from this denial of reality, refusing to equate the death penalty with the act of killing. Yet words are important. Even if they are right to assert that it is the *execution of* a sentence, it is undeniably also a homicide: "action of a human being who kills a human

---

203. Tocqueville (Alexis de), *Democracy in America*, Paris, Gallimard, 1986.

being"[204], which can be described with the verb *assassinate*: "to commit a premeditated homicide"[205]. These words strike fear into the hearts of pro-death penalty campaigners, who see them as an intrinsic expression of abolitionist militancy. As one woman we met in a restaurant on July 4th put it: "You don't have the right to use the word 'murder' for what the law calls 'execution'. It's a legal decision that has to be implemented." But these words are not wrong. They convey a reality that the retentionists don't want to admit publicly, while behind the scenes of the execution chambers, the administration in some states will write "*State-sanctioned* murder"[206] on the death certificate of the civil registry.

It would be pointless to end this reflection on a pessimistic note. As the abolitionist movement steadily gains the upper hand over national legislation, and as we see that even developing countries are succeeding in changing their criminal law, it is probable that, in the long term, the United States will not be able to continue isolating itself from the rest of the world by refusing to accept a major evolution in civilization. A global reputation is at stake, probably still imperceptible to the general public, but one that elected representatives, whether political or judicial at federal level, cannot reasonably persist in ignoring without measuring the consequences at diplomatic and international level.

In the United States, too, there are forces, enthusiasms and energies capable of moving mountains. The American abolitionist movement is small in numbers, but nevertheless vigorous. On the one hand, NGOs are doing remarkable work. Their activities are, after all, recent and have already won some victories. However, they must remain vigilant to the fact that the fight can only be won if we remain united behind an indivisible cause, whatever the cases put forward. For, in contrast

---

204. Larousse dictionary 2010.
205. Ibid.
206. State-sanctioned murder.

to a criticized criminal justice system, it is also around the integrity of abolitionist actors that the American population can envisage meeting. On the other side, teachers, researchers and a host of under-paid lawyers, often the last interlocutors of those forgotten on death row, work against the profit motive that has been established as a state religion. All of them turn their careers into a crusade for their country to change, for justice to legitimize its definition, and for humanity to triumph over barbarism. Everyone is aware that justice and the right to punish require a philosophical, cultural and ethical approach. This is the only way to distinguish this institution from the torture and arbitrary killing still practised by authoritarian regimes, which the United States is the first to denounce worldwide. It has to be said, however, that here or elsewhere, being a vigilante in one's own home is not always an easy ambition.

American justice, seen through the prism of capital punishment, describes an abyss haunted by a cohort of torments and sadisms that nothing can justify, not even security arguments. In the United States, there is a willingness to practice never-named tortures, authorized by the vagueness or severity of legal provisions, nurtured by a culture of violence and orchestrated by the immoral trades of a political and judicial world whose re-election feeds on the fears and desires for vengeance of a people cleverly left ignorant. Mass incarceration on the one hand, and conditions on death row on the other, cannot be the result of chance. The indifference of a nation of 300 million souls to the perpetuation of these inhumane practices, in the wake, moreover, of inequitable justice, necessarily has a meaning that society should discuss, seize upon, based on the certainty that there can be no process of civilization without the will to channel violence - both that of citizens and that of the State.

When history teaches us about the self-destructive madness of the human race, with the last century particularly zealous in terms of mass violence, be it the Nazi regime in Europe, the Khmer Rouge in

Cambodia, the Stalinists in Eastern Europe, the Maoists in China, or the many dictatorships skilfully scattered across Africa and Latin America, all these memories show us that mankind has no trouble devising systems to satisfy the political and economic supremacy of some, in defiance of the right to exist of others. At the same time, it is as if the last century had succeeded in making us admit that we have a common interest in combating all forms of violence perpetrated by ourselves against ourselves, and that we must remain vigilant in the face of the different faces which, behind so many perverse masks, make opinions and powers slide towards the justification of choices that our reason today knows to be unacceptable. From now on, there is a relationship with the mirror that the culture of human rights has taught us in particular, underlining the contours of a reflection necessarily carried out on the human species, leading us, *in fine, to* consider each of our fellow human beings as another self. Armed with the awareness that we are potentially violent animals, endowed with predatory talents that we know how to put to good use within our own species, humankind gradually decided that we would no longer eat each other: anthropophagy has disappeared from our societies. We have also decided that there is no hierarchy at the heart of our species, that sub-humans who can be cut and chopped at will, bartered and traded, are a notion to be outlawed: slavery is now relegated to the not-too-distant past. We will undoubtedly come to accept, on a universal scale, that no pretext or law can authorize us to kill each other. In fact, when it comes to justice, the question of universal abolition will leave the realm of opinion and enter the realm of evidence, which only criminals will attempt to challenge. This is the direction of our history, as we pursue a trajectory of impalpable energy, the timing and form of which we have no control over. This inescapable direction obeys a mystery that spans too many centuries to be qualified as temporal. In this way, we are gradually organizing our species and structuring our societies, despite the inertia and obstacles still posed today by a few reluctant individuals, like a last desperate breath.

In this expectation, we are also aware that the domestication of violence opens the way to possible loves, unhoped-for agreements, positive associations, enthusiasms to be discovered and met, endless exchanges with adventurous effects, and a whole range of emotions that make individual existences so many collective journeys dotted with oases. On a broader level, the aim is gradually to change the standard of thinking regarding the moral and legal acceptance of the violence permitted at the heart of the human species. This is the highly symbolic significance of the worldwide abolitionist movement, of this civilizational struggle that must urgently be extrapolated beyond the fight against the emblematic legalized killing of a few thousand individuals a year. In light of the advances made in previous centuries, it is incumbent on our contemporary generations to relentlessly develop a critical reflection on the legitimacy and use of confinement, as well as on all other forms of coercion, control, constraint and punishment. This is the accessible ambition of a new century.

BIBLIOGRAPHY

Books

Atwood (David), *Detour to Death Row*, Texas, Peacecenter Book Publisher, 2008.

Chessman (Caryl), *Cell 2455 Death Row*, 1954; *Cell 2455 Death Row*;
- *Trial by Ordeal*, 1955; *Through the Bars*;
- *The Face of Justice*, 1957;
- *The Kid Was a Killer*, 1960; *Son of Hate*.

Christie (Nils), *L'Industrie de la punition. Prison and penal policy in the West*, Paris, Autrement, 2003.

Dow (David R.), *Executed on a Technicality. Lethal Injustice on America's Death Row*, Boston, Beacon Press, 2005.
- *Autobiographie d'une exécution, Paris, Flammarion, 2010.*

Dow (Mark), *American Gulag: Inside U.S. Immigration Prisons*, Berkeley, Los Angeles, University of California Press, 2001.

Foucault (Michel), *Surveiller et punir*, Paris, Flammarion, 1975.

Gaillard (Arnaud), "La peine capitale au Burundi", in *La Peine de mort dans la région des Grands Lacs*, Paris, ECPM, 2007.
- *Sexualité et prison, désert affectif et désirs sous contrainte*, Paris, Max Milo, 2009.

Goffman (Erving), *Stigmate, les usages sociaux des handicaps*, Paris, Éditions de Minuit, coll. "Le Sens commun", 1975.

GUILLAUMAUD-PUJOL (Claude), *Chroniques de Philadelphie, Mumia Abu-Jamal, un homme libre dans le couloir de la mort*, Paris, Le Temps des cerises, 2007.

- *The Move case in Philadelphia 1975-1995. Fait divers ou événement historique*, doctoral thesis, 2000.

JACQUIN (Philippe), ROYOT (Daniel), WHITFIELD (Stephen), *Le Peuple américain, origines, immigrations, ethnicité et identité*, Paris, Éditions du Seuil, 2000.

KUPERS (Terry), *Prison Madness, the Mental Health Crisis Behind Bars and What We Must Do about It*, San Francisco, Jossey-Bass Publisher, 1999.

PELKE (Bill), *Journey of Hope... From Violence to Healing*, Bern Boerman, 2003.

PREJEAN (Sister Helen), *Dead Man Walking: An Eyewitness Account of the Death Penalty in the United States*, New York, Vintage Books, A division of Random House Inc., 1994.

- *Would Jesus Pull the Switch?"*, Salt of the Earth, March/April 1997.

RIVKIND (Nina) and SHATZ (Steven F.), *Cases and Materials on the Death Penalty*, 3rd edition, Saint Paul, Minnesota, American Press Book Series, West Academic Publishing, 2009.

STREIB (Victor L.), *Death Penalty for Female Offenders*, Ohio Northern University, 2009.

TOCQUEVILLE (Alexis de), *Democracy in America*, Paris, Gallimard, 1986.

TUROW (Scott), *Ultimate Punishment, a Lawyer's Reflection on Dealing with the Death Penalty*, New York, Farrar, Straus and Giroux Publisher, 2003.

WEBER (Max), *The Theory of Social and Economic Organization*, New York, The Free Press, 1st edition, 1964.

WILLETT (Jim) and ROZELLE (Ron), *Warden*, Albany, Bright Sky Press, 2004.

Articles and reports

ALEXANDER (Michelle), *The New Jim Crow: Mass Incarceration in the Age of Colorblindness*, New York, New Press Edition, Fall 2009.

DIETER (Richard C.), *A Crisis in Confidence, Americans' Doubts about the Death Penalty*, report by the Death Penalty Information Center, based on a national opinion poll, June 2007.

EFRATI (Amir), "Legal system struggles with how to react when police officers lie", *Wall Street Journal*, January 29 2009.

HARGROVE (Thomas), "Unsolved homicide rate climbs in U.S.", *Times Records News*, Wichita Falls, Texas, May 24, 2010.

HOPPE (C.), "Executions cost Texas millions", *The Dallas Morning News*, March 8, 1992.

JAMES (Randy), "A brief history of prison riots", *Time Magazine*, Tuesday August 11, 2009.

KIRBY (R.), "Executioners share motives, describe their roles in death by firing squad", *Salt Lake Tribune*, June 2010.

LANIEL (Laurent), *Alternatives internationales*, n° 6, January/February 2003.

LIPTAK (Adam), "1 in 100,000 U.S. adults behind bars, new study says", *New York Times*, February 28, 2008.

MILLS (Steve), "Cameron Todd Willingham case: Expert says fire for which father was executed was not arson", *Chicago Tribune*, August 25, 2009.

SCHWARTZ (John) and FITZSIMMONS (Emma G.), "Illinois governor signs capital punishment ban", *New York Times*, May 9, 2011.

TEMPEST (Rone), "Death row often means a long life", *Los Angeles Times*, March 6, 2005.

WAGNER (John) and AGIESTA (Jennifer), "Md. voters remain divided on death penalty", *Washington Post*, May 11, 2010.

Report by the International Centre for Prison Studies, King's College London, 2005.

Scattered Justice: Geographic Disparities of the Death Penalty, ACLU, March 5, 2004.

"Abandonment of thiopental production: a victory for ECPM and the Coalition", *Journal de l'abolition*, December 2010.

Facts about the Death Penalty, Death Penalty Information Center, updated December 17, 2010.

Death Row USA, NAACP Legal Defense & Educational Fund, Winter 2010.

"Mental illness, human rights, and U.S. prisons", Human Rights Watch statement for the record to the Senate Judiciary Committee Subcommittee on Human Rights and the Law, September 22, 2009.

Report of the Council to the Membership of the American Law Institute on the Matter of the Death Penalty, April 15, 2009.

"David Powell, model prisoner, to be executed 30 years after his conviction", Le Monde.fr with AFP, June 15, 2010.

"American gulag", *Washington Post*, May 26, 2005.

"Death no more", *Dallas Morning News*, April 18, 2007.

Electronic sources

Death Penalty Information Center (www.deathpenaltyinfo.org).

The StandDown Texas Project (www.standdown.typepad.com).

Surveys and polls

Gallup Poll, May 2006.

Gallup Poll, October 2009.

National Poll of Police Chiefs Puts Capital Punishment at Bottom of Law Enforcement Priorities, Death Penalty Information Center, 2009.

Males Arrests, by Age, 2004, Table 39, FBI.

US Census Bureau.

Crime in the United States 2008 - Department of Justice, FBI, (USA), September 2009, June 16, 2010.

Intentional Homicide Rate, UNDATA 2008.

Death Penalty Sentencing, United States General Accounting Office, February 1990.

Court decisions and institutional publications

"U.S. Supreme Court Roper v. Simmons," 543 U.S. 551 (2005).

"Soering v. United Kingdom", 11 Eur. Ct. H.R. (ser. A) (1989).

"Herrera v. Collins", 506 U.S. 390 (1993).

Preamble to Recommendation Rec(2006)2 of the Committee of Ministers to Member States on the European Prison Rules, adopted by the Council of Ministers on January 11, 2006.

Texas Administrative Code, title XXXVII, part IX, chapter CCLXXXV, rule 285-1.

Anti-Terrorism and Effective Death Penalty Act (AEDPA) of 1996.

INDEX OF KEY PEOPLE MENTIONED

1. Abu-Ali Abdur Rahman is a 60-year-old African-American man scheduled for execution in Tennessee on June 18, 2003. He was sentenced to death in 1987 for the murder of Patrick Daniels on February 17, 1986. On June 6, 2003, Abu-Ali was granted a stay of execution by the U.S. Court of Appeals for the 6th Circuit, 36 hours before his scheduled execution. He has spent 39 years of his life in prison. There is evidence that he has suffered from traumatic anxiety since childhood, when he was diagnosed with behavioral and post-traumatic stress disorders.

2. A. R. is 63 years old. He has been imprisoned in Parchman, Mississippi, for 11 years. He has been sentenced to death for a crime he claims he never committed. He is demanding DNA tests to clear his name. He was a cab driver in New Orleans. Today, he suffers from heart disease. His wife died while he was on death row. He was not previously opposed to the death penalty.

3. Barb Kirk is one of Veldean Kirk's daughters. A mother, she lives in the suburbs of Salt Lake City. She accompanies her mother on the night of the execution of Ronnie Lee Gardner, her father Nick's assailant, but does not attend the execution.

4. Brandie Gardner is the daughter of Ronnie Lee Gardner, executed on June 17, 2010 by firing squad at Salt Lake City State Prison, Utah. She attended her father's execution.

5. Cliff Johnson is a public defender in Jackson, Mississippi. A Columbia graduate, he was the attorney for Bobby Glen Wilcher, who was executed on October 18, 2006.

6. Curtis McCarty is 49 years old. He was exonerated and released in 2007 after spending 22 years in prison, 19 of them on death row - for a murder he didn't commit in Oklahoma in 1982. McCarty was tried twice and sentenced to death three times because of prosecutorial malpractice and the testimony of forensic scientist Joyce Chilchrist, whose forensic work helped secure at least two other wrongful convictions that were later overturned by DNA testing. The entire prosecution was based on a forensic lie and the falsification of an official FBI report, with the complicity of the District Attorney, the prosecutor and the judge. To avoid scandal, the forensic scientist who perpetrated the perjury was not prosecuted. Curtis was exonerated in 2007 thanks to the Innocence Project, but has still not been compensated for the damage he suffered as a result of this corruption of the judiciary. Since then, he has been involved in the abolitionist movement, speaking at conferences and as a photographer. He took part in the documentary film *HONK*[207] about the death penalty in the United States.

7. E.M. is a 37-year-old African-American. He spent 11 years incarcerated, including 5 on death row in Parchman, Mississippi, for a murder he has always denied. He was a truck driver. He has three children who "miss him terribly". Previously pro-death penalty, he now realizes the dysfunctions of American justice.

8. David Atwood is a retired oil company engineer. He spent more than 15 years working for the abolition of the death penalty in Texas. He is the founder of the Texas Coalition to Abolish the Death Penalty. A devout

---

207. *HONK*: documentary film on the death penalty in the United States, directed in 2010 by Arnaud Gaillard and Florent Vassault, produced by Andolfi and Centrale électrique, with the support of the association Ensemble contre la peine de mort (ECPM).

Catholic, he helps his spiritual community promote abolition. He is also the author of *Detour to Death Row.*

9. Debra Saunders is a reporter for the *San Francisco Chronicle.* Her column, published three times a week, is also picked up nation-wide and on townhall.com. Perceived by some as a conservative Republican, Saunders regularly fights against the abolition of the death penalty.

10. Delia Perez Meyer joined the abolitionist movement nine years ago when her brother, Louis Castro Perez, was accused of murdering three of his best friends in September 1998. She is involved with Amnesty International, sits on the board of the Texas Moratorium Network, and works for the Campaign to End the Death Penalty as well as the National and Texas Coalition to Abolish the Death Penalty.

11. Dennis Longmire is a professor of criminology at Sam Houston University in Huntsville, Texas. He is a long-time opponent of the death penalty. For many years, he has stood in front of the walls of Huntsville's Walls Prison at every execution to demonstrate his opposition to this legalized crime. "I've stood here with a candle more than 450 times, which is also more than 450 executions," he says.

12. Gloria Goodwin-Killian was released from prison on August 8, 2002 after serving 17.5 years of a 32-year sentence for a crime she had not committed. Initially, the death penalty had been requested. During her trial and incarceration, she always maintained her innocence. Today, she is the executive director of a non-profit association she founded, the Action Committee for Women in Prison (ACWIP), to support women in prison.

13. Golda Medina is the mother of death row inmate Tony Medina, locked up for 15 years on Polunsky's death row in Livingston, Texas. Golda fights for a new trial for her son. For the richness of her speech and the charisma that emanates from her simplicity,

Golda participates in artistic creations in favor of abolition. She was photographed by Caroline Planque and featured in the documentary *HONK*.

14. Hank Skinner has been on death row in Texas since he was convicted of a triple murder in 1995. He has always denied his guilt, yet the courts have always refused to allow him to prove his innocence through DNA testing. In March 2011, he obtained permission from the US Supreme Court to request DNA testing *via* civil proceedings. He is married to and supported by Sandrine Ageorges-Skinner, a French activist deeply committed to the abolitionist movement.

15. James G. Rytting is an attorney in Houston, Texas. He concentrates primarily on representing his clients in their state and federal appeals. In habeas corpus proceedings, Mr. Rytting has successfully argued a number of death row cases. He was counsel for Jonathan Marcus Green, for whom he obtained a stay of execution in June 2010.

16. Jamie and Tammy Stewart are the granddaughters and daughters of Veldean Kirk. Their grandfather and father was stabbed to death by Ronnie Lee Gardner in 1985. He had survived his wounds, but his health had become fragile and he died 10 years later. Jamie attended Ronnie's execution by firing squad on June 18, 2010 in Salt Lake City.

17. Jay Gross is pastor of Southern Baptist Church in Conroe, Texas. He graduated from the University of Houston (1976) and became Doctor of Ministry in 1986 at Southwestern Baptist Theological Seminary.

18. Jeanne Woodford is the former Warden of San Quentin Prison in California (the first woman to hold this position), and the former Director of the California Department of Corrections. She is now Executive Director of the abolitionist association Death Penalty Focus. The mother of a large family, she has always been opposed to the death penalty, although her duties have led her to be respon-

sible for carrying out four executions. Today, she campaigns for alternative sentences and social measures to reduce crime rates.

19. Jessica Mederson is a young lawyer at Vinson & Elkins LLP in Austin, Texas. For the first time in her career, she agrees to work on a criminal case on a *pro bono* basis, to defend Michael Perry, a young man sentenced to death, and conduct his final appeals after his initial conviction. Michael was finally executed on July 1st, 2010 in Huntsville, Texas.

20. Jim Willett is the former warden of Walls Prison in Huntsville, Texas. Jim supervised 89 executions before retiring. He began his career as a simple guard and ended up as warden of the famous Walls prison in Huntsville, where the majority of executions in the United States take place. He is now director of the Huntsville Prison Museum.

21. Jo McCarty is retired from the Navy and General Motors. He is the father of Curtis McCarty, exonerated after 22 years on death row in Oklahoma. Jo claims to be a patriot, to have lived the American Dream, and now spends his retirement in a nice American middle-class subdivision. However, his son's judicial career has opened his eyes to the many lies governing his country's judicial life and the corruptions in the police system.

22. Jordan Smith is a journalist with the *Austin Chronicle*, specializing in judicial and political affairs. In particular, she is an expert on the analysis of dysfunctions in the American justice system.

23. Kent Scheidegger has been legal director of the Criminal Justice Foundation in Sacramento since 1986. He has written over 100 death penalty appeals for the U.S. Supreme Court. He is an ardent advocate of the death penalty as a necessary solution to crime in his country.

24. Kevin Cooper is a 55-year-old African-American, incarcerated at San Quentin Penitentiary in California, on death row for 25

years. He had previously been incarcerated and escaped from other prisons. He is accused of a triple murder, which he has always denied. His guilt is the subject of much controversy.

25. Lindy Lou Wells is a *middle-class* Mississippi mother. Her conservative, Republican views were destined to make her a pro-death penalty advocate, until she attended the trial of Bobby Glen Wilcher. Forced to vote for a death sentence by the other members of the jury, she began a correspondence with him and became his only friend. She realized how dangerous the death penalty was and how dysfunctional the courts were, and became an abolitionist.

26. Mumia Abu-Jamal is an African-American journalist and activist. He was a member of the Black Panther movement. In 1982, he was sentenced to death for the murder of Daniel Faulkner, a Philadelphia police officer. Innocent for some, in self-defense for others, his conviction scandalized international opinion. A worldwide mobilization for his release and/or a new trial took place. He has become a symbol for many opponents of capital punishment. He has been on death row in Pittsburgh prison for 29 years, from where he continues to write about American politics and society.

27. Norman C. Hile, a partner in Orrick's Sacramento office, is a business lawyer. On a *pro bono* basis, he is Kevin Cooper's criminal defense attorney for his appeals.

28. Patricia Lykos is the former Chief Judge of the Harris County Criminal Courts, where she presided over more than 20,000 trials during 14 years. She was a professor at South Texas College of Law and taught at the National Judicial College. In 2002, she was appointed by Governor Rick Perry to the Governor's Council on Sex Offender Treatment. Today, she is the District Attorney for Harris County, corresponding to the city of Houston, Texas. Prior to her election, this was the county with the highest number of death sentences in the state. She remains in favor of the death penalty, but proposes a more moderate use of the death penalty.

29. Rick Halperin is Director of the Human Rights Education Program at Southern Methodist University in Dallas. He has served on the boards of several associations, including the National Coalition to Abolish the Death Penalty (NCADP), Human Rights Initiative, Capital Punishment Investigation and Education Services, and others. Since 1972, he has been very active in efforts to abolish the death penalty in the United States. He works with numerous abolitionist associations, criminal lawyers, representatives of several religions, editorial directors, victims' rights groups and others. He is a past president of the Texas Coalition to Abolish the Death Penalty (TCADP). He was elected to chair Amnesty International's Executive Board from 1992 to 1993. Today, he is a board member of Journey of Hope… From Violence to Healing.

30. Robert R. Bryan, a San Francisco criminal lawyer, has been lead counsel on a wide range of criminal cases, specializing in death row cases. He is a member of the bar of the U.S. Supreme Court, California, New York, Alabama, and several federal courts. He is past president of the National Coalition to Abolish the Death Penalty. In 2003, Mr. Bryan agreed to represent Mumia Abu-Jamal. This collaboration will conclude at the end of 2010. Mr. Bryan represents capital defendants in state and federal courts, and has defended numerous defendants against whom the death penalty has been sought.

31. Sandrine Ageorges-Skinner is a French activist who has been campaigning against the death penalty for many years. She is a film production director and co-wrote her first documentary on the death penalty in the United States, based on her personal and activist history with death row inmate Hank Skinner, with whom she has corresponded since 1996 and whose wife she became. She is also deeply involved in the American and international abolitionist movements, nurturing a very precise expertise on the diversity of penal mechanisms in each state. She is a board member of the association Ensemble contre la peine de mort, which she

represents on the steering committee of the World Coalition Against the Death Penalty.

32. Steve Hall is the director of the StandDown Texas Project, which he founded, an association dedicated to identifying and promoting best practices in the criminal justice system. He served as Texas Attorney General's right-hand man from 1983 to 1991, and as Administrator of the Texas Resource Center from 1993 to 1995. He has worked for the U.S. Congress and several elected officials in Texas, then as a public relations consultant for the private sector, non-profit associations and political figures. He also served as communications director for two political campaigns in Texas. A former journalist, he has received awards from the Associated Press Texas for his investigative work.

33. Steven Kreytak is a reporter for the *Austin American-Stateman*. In particular, he covers court cases.

34. Steven Shatz is a university professor and director of the Keta Taylor Colby Capital Punishment Project at the University of San Francisco, founded in 2001 to involve law students in interim reform and the process of abolishing the death penalty in the United States. He oversees the Southern Internship Program, which sends students each summer to work with criminal lawyers in the southern United States. He has been a lecturer at UC Berkeley, and a visiting professor at the East China Institute teaching politics and law in Shanghai, as well as at UC Hastings School of Law. With his wife, Nina Rivkind, he wrote *Dossiers et matériaux sur la peine de mort*.

35. T. M. is a 35-year-old man who has been incarcerated on Texas death row for 16 years for a crime he claims not to have committed. He was convicted of killing a brother and sister on New Year's Eve. In fact, he believes that, as the ex-leader of a Houston gang, the police wanted to neutralize him. His trial seems to have been an example of judicial dysfunction. Defense witnesses were not heard.

36. T. P. is a 25-year-old African-American man. Father of one, he was a salesman and lumber deliveryman for building houses. He has been on death row in Parchman, Mississippi, for four years for participating in a burglary in which a man died. He has made five different confessions, without ever admitting exactly what it is that has earned him his death sentence.

37. Veldean Kirk, 78, was born in Hollywood and followed her family to Utah as a teenager. She married Nick Kirk, a policeman, and they had three children. Her husband died 10 years after being shot in 1985 by Ronnie Lee Gardner while on duty. She attended Ronnie Lee Gardner's execution on June 17, 2010 in Salt Lake City, Utah. Veldean is also a character in the documentary film *HONK*.

38. William Redick is an attorney in Nashville, Tennessee. He is Abu-Ali Abdur Rahman's lawyer and friend. For several years, he has been trying to get the courts to accept the commutation of his death sentence to time served.

39. W. M. is a 43-year-old African-American who has been held on death row in Parchman, Mississippi, for 17 years. He has long maintained his innocence. He is accused of participating in a burglary during which four people died. W. M. is poor and uneducated. He spent his time in prison studying American criminal law and defended his own life in court. He proved that he could not have been at the scene of the crime at the time of the murders. The court accepted some of his objections. In March 2006, the court overturned its own decision, but he remains on death row. The possibility of his execution remains a reality, and he is now working on the ultimate opportunity to prove his innocence.

Aknowledgments

This study was carried out with the help of Florent Vassault and Émile Carreau, both of whom I would like to thank sincerely. They were my daily collaborators in bringing this research work to fruition, sharing as we went along the many questions that the sometimes aggressive and violent encounter with the reality of capital punishment in the United States inevitably raised.

I would also like to thank Sandrine Ageorges-Skinner, tireless activist and wife of death row inmate Hank Skinner, whose insight has regularly enriched this analysis. Thanks to Claude Guillaumaud-Pujol, activist, researcher and author specializing in American civilization. In addition to their talents as translators, they accompanied and guided my interrogations on the death penalty in the United States. Thanks also to Fabrice Ferrier for his faith and constant support in my projects.

Finally, I'd like to thank the association Ensemble contre la peine de mort (ECPM) and its team of employees and volunteers, for placing their trust in me and, above all, for the strength of their faith in the universal abolition of the death penalty, which must now be completed. Their commitment, humble and selfless, remains an essential and effective lever in this battle for civilization.

This essay frequently draws on the work of abolitionists in the United States, more specifically the Death Penalty Information Center and the StandDown Texas Project. The data collected is due to the generosity of all the people I have met: lawyers, journalists, activists, victims' families, researchers, death row inmates, etc. All of them have accepted my many curiosities, formulated by as many questions as questions. They all accepted my many curiosities and questions about the maintenance of capital punishment in a democracy such as the United States, a vast nation that prides itself on placing freedom among its founding values. The road to abolition has been embarked upon by the American people. Let's hope that justice, in the light of an accessible horizon, will find the means to no longer abuse its primary definition.

Among the many contributors who inspired this field survey, special thanks go to: Abu-Ali Abdur Rahman, Alan Rubenstein, Andre de Gruy, Barbara Becnel, Bettye Wilkinson, Bob Walden, Brandie Gardner, Cliff Johnson, Crystal Bybee, Curtis and Jo McCarty, David Atwood, David P. Weeks, David Voisin, Debra Saunders, Delia Perez, Dennis Longmire, Eric Moffett, Gloria Goodwin-Killian, Gloria Rubac, Golda and Tony Medina, James Rytting, Jamie and Tammy Stewart, Jay Gross, Jeanne Woodford, Jessica Mederson, Jim Willett, Jordan Smith, Kent Scheidegger, Kevin Cooper, Ricky Bell, Lindy Lou Wells, Mumia Abu-Jamal, Norman Hile, Patricia Lykos, Rick Halperin, Robert R. Bryan, Roderick Green, Roy Sanders, Steve Hall, Steven Kreytak, Steven Shatz, Terry Pitchford, Veldean, Mandy and Barb Kirk, William Redick, Willie Manning.

TABLE OF CONTENTS

Best sellers Max Milo Editions

Hitler's banker, Jean-François Bouchard

Confessions of a forger, Éric Piedoie Le Tiec

The Koran and the flesh, Ludovic-Mohamed Zahed

Governing by fake news, Jacques Baud

Governing by chaos, Collectif

A political history of food, Paul Ariès

Mad in U.S.A.: The ravages of the "American model",
Michel Desmurget

Mondial soccer club geopolitics, Kévin Veyssière

Putin: Game master?, Jacques Braud

Treatise on the three impostors: Moses, Jesus, Muhammad,
The Spirit of Spinoza

TV Lobotomy, Michel Desmurget